Dal & Rice

Footprints Series
JANE ERRINGTON, Editor

The life stories of individual women and men who were participants in interesting events help nuance larger historical narratives, at times reinforcing those narratives, at other times contradicting them. The Footprints series introduces extraordinary Canadians, past and present, who have led fascinating and important lives at home and throughout the world.

The series includes primarily original manuscripts but may consider the English-language translation of works that have already appeared in another language. The editor of the series welcomes inquiries from authors. If you are in the process of completing a manuscript that you think might fit into the series, please contact her, care of McGill-Queen's University Press, 3430 McTavish Street, Montreal, QC H3A 1X9.

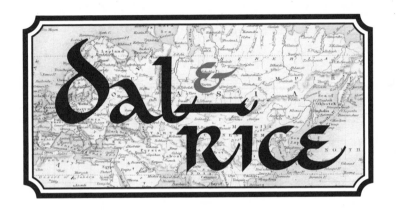

WENDY M. DAVIS

McGILL-QUEEN'S UNIVERSITY PRESS

MONTREAL & KINGSTON · LONDON · ITHACA

© McGill-Queen's University Press 2009

ISBN 978-0-7735-3432-2

Legal deposit first quarter 2009
Bibliothèque nationale du Québec

Printed in Canada on acid-free paper that
is 100% ancient forest free (100% post-
consumer recycled), process chlorine free.

McGill-Queen's University Press acknowl-
edges the support of the Canada Council for
the Arts for our publishing program. We also
acknowledge the financial support of the
Government of Canada through the Book
Publishing Industry Development Program
(BPIDP) for our publishing activities.

**Library and Archives Canada Cataloguing
in Publication**

Davis, Wendy M. (Wendy Marion), 1928–
Dal and rice / Wendy M. Davis.

(Footprints series ; 9)
ISBN 978-0-7735-3432-2

1. Davis, Wendy M. (Wendy Marion),
1928– –Childhood and youth. 2. Davis,
Wendy M. (Wendy Marion), 1928–
–Family. 3. Davis, Godfrey. 4.
India–Biography.
I. Title. II. Series.

DS481.D3643A3 2009
954.03'5092
C2008-903947-5

This book was designed and typeset by
studio oneonone in Sabon 10.2/14

Image on vi: Two painted wooden
musicians, made in Moradabad, India,
and bought in Edmonton.

I dedicate this book to a bridge of friendship between Canada, Great Britain, India, Pakistan, Burma, Tibet, and Afghanistan. And to all the songbirds of the world.

Contents

Acknowledgments

My acknowledgments tell a story of why I have a great love for India and make me realize how many people and experiences contribute to everyone's lives. I apologize for those I have forgotten to acknowledge; they too are near and dear to me.

As a form of acknowledgment, royalties from the sale of *Dal and Rice* will go to Seva, an organization in Vancouver that provides medical aid to Tibet, Nepal, and India; and to Shreyas, Leena Sarabhai's school in Ahmedabad, India.

Coming to Canada uprooted me and gave me the necessary distance from India, compelling me to write about my childhood. The years have passed so quickly. Now that I am retired, I am fortunately able to continue enjoying life and its wonders. I would love to hear stories from the readers of this book and renew old friendships. As

I reflect on the passing of the years, I think of antique dealers who make the best husbands, because in their view the older you get the more interesting you become.

My thanks to those who focused on my writing:

Rachael Kilsonk, who corrected my writing when I took a correspondence course with Alberta Culture.

Eunice Scarfe, who was my teacher when I retired and attended the Spring Session for Seniors organized by the Extension Department, University of Alberta, later ELLA, the Edmonton Lifelong Learners' Association.

Shirley Serviss, whose class I attended at Spring Session for Seniors.

My writing group, which was an offshoot of Eunice's class and has been running for ten years, thanks to Joyce Harries.

Margaret Macpherson, who critiqued an early draft of my manuscript.

Glen Huser, author and writer-in-residence at ELLA, who gave me encouragement after reading my manuscript.

Yvonne Brown, librarian at the Edmonton Public Library who located Lord Wavell's poetry anthology *Other Mens' Flowers*, and John Riddick's *Who's Who in British India* (1998).

Shelagh Wildsmith, who is irreplaceable and who helps me organize my life and keep my manuscript in one box.

Anita Petrinjak, a writing colleague, for her expertise on the computer.

Shaun Cooney for unfailing help with my computer.

Jill McIvor, who came especially from Salt Spring Island to help me with the final selection of photographs for my manuscript.

Lesley Latta-Guthrie, director of the Provincial Archives of Alberta, who willingly gave me her expertise in selecting the photographs for my manuscript.

Katie Roth, reprographic technician at the Provincial Archives of
  Alberta.
Tim Bowling, writer-in-residence for the Canadian Authors Associa-
  tion, who suggested sending three chapters of my manuscript to
  many publishers, including McGill-Queen's University Press.
Leena Sarabhai, who invited me to stay with her and her family
  in India.
Barbara Chamberlain, without whose expertise and unfailing help
  this manuscript would never have been completed.
Joyce Seys-Phillips, my sister, and Catherine Wedderburn, Joyce's
  granddaughter, for giving me helpful information.
Joan Harcourt, editor, McGill-Queen's University Press, whose editorial
  experience enabled this manuscript to live again. It was languishing,
  but having nine lives like a cat, it recovered. My heartfelt gratitude.
Joan McGilvray, who kept the manuscript gently moving along; Claire
  Gigantes, my co-editor, who sympathetically pruned my manuscript;
  and the wonderful team at McGill-Queen's University Press.
Prof. Donna Clanfield and Shelagh Wildsmith for kindly proofreading.

Thanks to those who helped me indirectly with *Dal and Rice*:

The Burmah Oil Company, where I worked as a secretary for
  G.F. Wilson, a geologist.
Aline McNaughton, who employed me at the Princess Margaret
  Orthopaedic Hospital, Edinburgh, as a newly graduated occupational
  therapist.
Two Calgarian physiotherapists, Mary McKnight (Cornes) and Ruth
  Goodchild, whom I had the good luck to work with at the Edin-
  burgh Royal Infirmary. My father was at peace; he had died and
  I was free to travel and fulfill my dream to emigrate to Canada.
Photographs of the Rockies reminded me of the Himalayas and

Kashmir. Mary and Ruth suggested that I apply to the Faculty of
Rehabilitation Medicine, Department of Occupational Therapy,
University of Alberta, as a teaching assistant. I was successful thanks
to Professor L. Albon.

Grey Owl, whom I met as a child in Sussex, England, and who
enthralled me with his stories of beaver in Canada.

Denise and Christopher Amery, who found Edmonton on a map,
decided that it was flat and cold, that there would be lots of snow,
and that I must take cross-country skis with me. They also gave me
the pleasure of a goddaughter, Susanna.

Penny Plain, a dress shop in Edinburgh that always gave me pleasure
because they sold dresses made from Indian prints.

England's Department for International Development, which sends
me pension cheques for which I am grateful.

Yvonne Grandison, Bank of Scotland, Shandwick Place, Edinburgh,
who helps me with transatlantic money issues.

Hilda Priestly, the wife of an army officer stationed in India and a
great friend, now dead, who encouraged me in my writing.

David and Sarah Gilmour of Edinburgh, who shared their writing
expertise with me.

Isobel Reid, who critiqued my manuscript in its early life.

Marjorie Guthrie, who encouraged me to attend the Edinburgh Book
Festival and hear wonderful Indian authors.

Dr Gilliam Evison, Librarian at the Indian Institute, Bodleian Library,
Oxford, who made my manuscript available for student research.

Gloria Sawai, a teacher of writing and winner of the Governor
General's Award.

Catrina Edwards, teacher of creative writing at the Spring Session
for Seniors.

The Banff Centre, where I attended a writing course.

Naomi Roberts, a very dear cousin who critiqued my manuscript.

The Edmonton branch of the Alpine Club, which enabled me to stay
at the Waites Gibson Cabin in the Tonquin Valley, which brought
back memories of Kashmir.

Robyn Short, who filed and indexed many of my Indian photographs
and who was an active member of Images Photographic Club.

Louise and Jean Fournet, who included me in family outings, with
Lucie and Marc, to the Rockies, which always brought back memories of the Himalayas and Kashmir.

Irenie Lau and family, neighbours who bring me delicious wonton
soup and encourage me with my writing. Thanks, too, to Yeng,
their relative, who accommodated Jill McIvor.

Heather, Bob, and Rory MacMillan, who keep my spirits up by
sharing family Sunday suppers with me.

Bob MacMillan for help with my computer.

Chantelle Leidl, who volunteered on an irrigation project in Gujarat.
When I was visiting Gandhi's ashram I was told that another Canadian had recently been working there; I was given Chantelle's
address in Canada and we became friends.

Grant Assenheimer, Chantelle's friend, who visited me on his bicycle
during a snowstorm, bringing me his homemade chocolate cookies.

Mustafa Siddiqi, a scholarship student from Afghanistan, also a friend
of Chantelle's, who treated us all to delicious Afghan curries at the
Ariana Afghan Restaurant.

Ten Thousand Villages, a Mennonite store that sells crafts, like my
wooden musicians, from around the world and sends the proceeds
directly to the makers.

Vivian Bosley, who lent me interesting books to read, relevant to India.

Helene Narayana, who shares Indian memories with me.

Lata and Bhupen Parekh, who invite me to their home to have special

dal and rice, also dokhla ground dal with ground rice, cooked
together.

Anju and Sirish Shah, who share their family with me.

The Devonian Botanic Gardens crafters' group who gave me enjoy-
ment working with pressed flowers, especially the blue poppy that
reminded me of Kashmir.

Dr C. Lord, my GP, who enables me to keep writing.

Dr G. Lavoie, who gave me a knee replacement, which enabled me
to be pain free and so keep writing.

Patricia and Jim Downing, who encouraged me with my earlier
writing relating to occupational therapy.

The Edmonton International Dancers, with whom I dance and enjoy
the music of other countries.

Lynne Fahlman, who shares her adventures of Northern India with me
and brought me a beautiful Indian shawl.

Tanzam Auto Centre, whose owner, Moez Khakoo, is like a medical
doctor with my old car.

The staff at the TD Bank, McKernan branch, who give me necessary
help and always with a smile.

Jonathan Sawatsky, Becky's son, who as a schoolboy helped me
purchase an Apple laptop computer and showed me how to use
it for my writing.

Marina Pershina, whose weekly visits to care for my canaries enabled
me to have writing time.

Northern Alberta Caged Bird Society, who enabled me to keep birds
of my childhood.

Diane Lyon and Yuri Drohomirecki, who shared their love of India
with me.

Camilla Gibb, writer-in-residence, University of Alberta, who encouraged me to complete my manuscript.

The staff at the Strathcona Post Office, Edmonton, who helped me
    with their expertise in expressing and registering my manuscript.
St Joseph's Hospital, Edmonton, where I worked, whose patients
    taught me about Canada.
Gira Sarabhai, curator of her family's textile museum in Ahmenabad,
    who gave me permission to read a file she had kept of my father and
    her father's letters extending over the fifty years of their friendship.
Stephen Woollcombe, who as a CUSO volunteer worked at Leena's
    school and shared his experiences with me.
Dr Brian Hill of Adelaide, Australia, and Wellington, New Zealand,
    who wrote his PhD on my grandfather, David Ziman.
John Horrigan of Antique Maps.
Jack Lamoureux at Scova Print and Copy, Edmonton, who is always
    helpful with my constant photocopying.
Mr Chapman, who worked with Tibetan refugees in India. Sadly he
    took his own life following the invasion of Tibet by the Chinese.
Charles Allen, author of *Plain Tales from the Raj*, whose book
    brought back many memories.
Rumer Godden, whose books made me appreciate her Indian childhood.
Mark Tulley, whose love of India as revealed in his books never ceases
    to give me pleasure.
William Dalrymple, whose books are a constant pleasure to read.
The Honourable Mrs Bruce, whose book *Peeps at Many Lands:
    Kashmir* brought back many good memories for me.
Rudyard Kipling, whose stories influenced my life.
Gerald Durrell, whose stories always give pleasure.

Indians all over the world have brought with them many wonders including their tasty curries. It is a treat to have curry, but my memories of India are always awakened by the less-appetizing dal and rice. In 2002, in Alberta, my friends Lata and Bhupen invited me and other friends to celebrate the Diwali, the Festival of Lights. Their friends all brought a delicious contribution to the dinner. Among the dishes was dokhla, ground dal with ground rice, cooked together – an exquisite dal and rice I had never before had that gave a new pleasure to eating those foods.

WENDY DAVIS
Edmonton, 2008

Wendy Davis, Sussex, 1947.

Foreword

It is a privilege to be asked to write this foreword for *Dal and Rice*, a wonderful pot-pourri of memories of a childhood in India. I have known Wendy and her sister, Joyce, since I was a boy when Wendy once drove me through Scotland in her battered red car. Joyce's son, Nigel, was one of my best friends and I was staying with the family on holiday in Perth. I can't remember where we were going at the time or why. But, inevitably, because I suspect Wendy is accident-prone, we broke down in one of the remoter parts of the Highlands.

For a teenager this was a huge adventure, though a little daunting as darkness was falling. Wendy exuded a great sense of calm as if she knew that someone would turn up and rescue us. Sure enough, right on cue, a local farmer arrived and after completing a few repairs sent us on our way. It all seemed very normal to Wendy. Forty years on, having read these memoirs, I finally understand why. For a child growing up in a household full of chatter and noise, laughter and tears in a land instinctively bracing itself for change, every day was an adventure. Something always turned up.

Wendy and I share a love of India and we also shared the love of an inspirational woman called Anne Ayres. Anne was an old-fashioned governess, a teacher more than a nanny. After her time with Wendy's family in India, Anne came into my family and stayed there for the next fifty years, though she retired from active duty in 1976. In recent years, Wendy would come over to England from her home in Canada and we would drive down to see Anne, who, though well into her nineties, had a memory as sharp as a pin. Wendy and Anne would reminisce about their time in India and I would listen. Perhaps these conversations proved an inspiration for *Dal and Rice*.

My own grandfather was the penultimate viceroy, Lord Wavell, who appears in some of the many stories in these pages. He died before I was born but would instantly have recognized the provincial India so evocatively drawn by Wendy. Wendy's father, Godfrey Davis – "Pa" – was a high court judge in the Indian Civil Service (ICS). After Independence, Lord Wavell spent much of the remaining years of his life campaigning on behalf of the ICS, whose work he respected so greatly. He thought the administrative foot soldiers of the ICS were the forgotten heroes of empire and tried to give them a voice in the corridors of power.

Wavell, a man of letters as well as of action, would also have sympathized with the dilemma that faced Wendy's father in the aftermath of the Salt March, organized by Mahatma Gandhi in protest against the tax recently imposed on salt. Pa had to do his duty and put Gandhi in prison, but he developed a friendship with the great man that lasted much longer than any political divisions. The story of Pa being summoned one morning in later years to meet Gandhi and his entourage at Poplar Tube Station, then escorting them on a day trip round London, stands as a tribute to Pa, the ICS, and the legacy of British rule in India.

Pa making a toast at the wedding of a cricket-playing friend: "This time John has bowled a beautiful maiden over." As Andrew notes, the British passed their love of cricket to the Indians, who excel at it. The game is a great leveller.

While Britain's civil servants were counting heads, carving out administrative districts, and establishing the basic electoral framework that makes India the most populous democracy in the world, their officers were fostering an equally enduring passion among Indians for the game of cricket. Inevitably, the imperial masters are now routinely humbled by their protégés, both in India and Australia, a compliment to the excellence of our tuition, of course.

As ever with Wendy, the following pages are alive with animals, a tangle of Indian wildlife and domestic pets. For a dedicated animal lover, India was heaven, even when monkeys invaded the bathroom and stole the soap and snakes caused pile-ups on the road. Any reader familiar with the exploits of Rikki Tikki Tavi, the fearless mongoose from Rudyard Kipling's *Jungle Book*, will recognize the scene in which a series of servants are summoned to dispose of a snake at the bottom of the garden and understand the mixture of excitement and fear that ran through the children of the house.

Dal and Rice is a delight, the result of a sharp eye, a good memory, and a real zest for life. It is a portrait of a lost age, probably rose-tinted, certainly seductive. It is part social history, part travelogue, but mostly a very personal account of a relationship with an exotic, chaotic, and often mysterious country. "This is India, you must expect these happenings," Wendy's mother used to say when a scorpion was found in a sandal or a snake found snoozing on the verandah. And this is India, the exotic and mysterious Wendy's India. I wish her well with the book.

ANDREW LONGMORE
Reigate, Surrey, UK
January 2008

Andrew Longmore, grandson of Lord Archibald P. Wavell, the penultimate Indian viceroy. The picture was taken at the ninetieth birthday of Anne Ayres, the beloved governess whom he and Wendy had in common.

Foreword

Ambalal Sarabhai was the hereditary owner of renowned textile mills in Ahmedabad, in the Indian state of Gujarat. He provided Mahatma Gandhi with much support. He also befriended a young Godfrey Davis when he, a "nobody," first arrived in Ahmedabad. Ambalal invited Godfrey and his newly wedded wife – the only white woman in Ahmedabad – to dinner, a significant gesture for the times, and all the more welcome for being unusual.

When Sir Godfrey was stationed in Ahmedabad, he lived very near my father Ambalal Sarabhai's house. I can't remember anyone more friendly and understanding – to children as well as adults. The years of intense conflict between the British and the Indians made no difference to his friendship with my father. When Sir Godfrey was moved to other positions, his relationship with my family not only continued but became

Leena Sarabhai at Shreyas, the school that she founded in Ahmedabad, Gujarat.
With her are two of her assistants.

stronger. He visited us every year. The children were always happy to see him, and birds he had tamed during earlier visits would follow him about. When I started a school, Sir Godfrey got involved: I can vividly recall his digging up a pond. He always brought gifts for the schoolchildren, which delighted them.

Sir Godfrey and my father had a long and flourishing correspondence and he also wrote to me. His daughter Wendy was a particular favourite with us and the link between the two families remains intact to this day because of her. Though I am at the moment unwell, making it difficult for me to do justice to the great Sir Godfrey, everyone who is interested in India and the colonial era should consider this book as an intimate picture of those times.

LEENA SARABHAI
Ahmedabad
15 January 2008

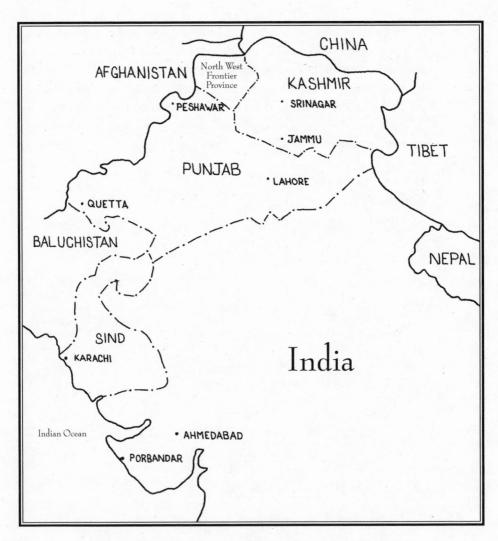

Sketch Map of British North India (1940)

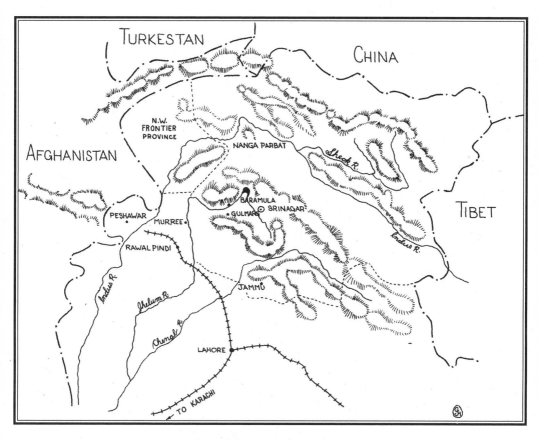

Sketch Map of Kashmir

Dal & Rice

One

❀

In the Beginning

Pa learned from the Indian people that a daughter resembled her mother not by her facial appearance but by her behind. Mother and daughter could be recognized when their behinds were identical. If this was true, presumably my father liked his future mother-in-law since mother and daughter had similar behinds.

My mother, Bessie Ziman, was born in 1895 to David and Lena Ziman in Reefton, New Zealand. David Ziman was a financier and prominent mining entrepreneur. He moved his family to England when my mother was a girl. They lived in London in the house opposite the one where my father grew up and my parents had been childhood friends. When they were teenagers my father would signal to my mother by hanging a white pillow slip out of the window. This was an invitation to go for a walk in the late afternoon, the closest thing to romance that the two young people achieved.

Grandfather David Ziman as a young man. I do not know who made this portrait.

Below left and right: My maternal grandparents, David and Lena Ziman.

Bessie Ziman, my mother.

My mother always appreciated her piano teacher, Tobias Matthay, who was known, among other things, for his books on piano technique.

As a girl my mother learned the piano and studied in London under Tobias Matthay.[1] She thought very highly of him and she was evidently an excellent student. My mother told me that she had had a crush on a conductor, Basil Henriques. She and her great friend Nelly Gaster would sit in the front row at the Albert Hall so that she could watch every movement he made and idolize him from nearby. She also enjoyed going to piano recitals given by Myra Hess, who was then a young woman like herself.[2]

When war was declared in 1914 my mother joined the land army. She was proud of the fact that she had worked as a dairymaid for the Queen's Dairy Herd at Windsor. Working on the land was hard on the hands. My mother, being a pianist, was trained to take good care of her hands and the head dairyman was shocked one day to find a nail file in the cows' bran. "Who owns this?" he demanded. My mother, pink with embarrassment, owned up. She was mortified that her nail file had fallen out of her uniform pocket into the bran. I know that she was reprimanded and that her punishment was not being allowed to deliver milk to the king and queen at Windsor Castle, which had been part of her duties. My mother also sang in the choir at Windsor Castle conducted by Sir Walter Parratt, Master of the King's Music.[3] On Sundays the choir members were sometimes invited to take tea with the king and queen at the castle.

My mother developed great respect for farmers. They could never have an extra hour in bed because the cows had to be milked. The crops had to be tended daily. In the land army the hoe was my mother's constant companion as she worked large acres of turnip and other crops. She also had to wear an ugly khaki-coloured uniform so there was no forgetting that there

My mother, Bessie Ziman, in the Land Army, working at the queen's dairy farm at Windsor, 1914. The horse was used on the farm.

was a war raging. My mother had a large collection of interesting brass buttons. I asked her where they came from and she explained, "From my boyfriends." Most of her friends were in the services and when they came home on leave they went down to Windsor to visit her. To make sure that she would not forget them they would pull off one of their uniform buttons and give it to her as a keepsake. This was evidently the custom. The services must have had quite a time replacing all those lost brass buttons.

After the war my mother was delighted to leave her land army job. No longer would she have to get up in the dark, eat heavy food with the farm-hands, or share an oil lamp at bedtime. The choir was her only pleasure, as she had been unable to practise the piano. Now she was able to return to her one special challenge of becoming a concert pianist.

Pa, on the other hand, had nothing but challenges in training for his career.

My paternal grandfather was a builder in London. My father, his eld-est son, was born on 23 October 1890. Pa spent his school holidays as an apprentice bricklayer in his father's company. One day while my grandfa-ther was showing a prospective client around a site the man noticed Pa working. He asked who the handsome intelligent-looking bricklayer was. My grandfather acknowledged that it was his son. Grandpa assumed that Pa would carry on the family business, but my father had different dreams. He was blessed with a brilliant mind and after attending a business school in Germany he realized that being a builder could not be his life's work. He studied at the Slade School of Art in London and also won a scholar-ship to Cambridge University. He entered Clare College where he ob-tained a first-class degree in law. His don said there was only one place for a mind as brilliant as his and that was the Indian Civil Service. After coming down from Cambridge he attended the Inns of Court where he ar-ticled with Lloyd George, who later became prime minister. When it came

Grandpa Davis, an
alderman of London.

to passing the law exams a favourite saying of Pa's was "Many are called
but few are chosen." As far as my father was concerned women had no
place among the chosen few. He felt that women's squeaky voices lowered
the standard and that painted nails and faces were not acceptable in the
courtroom. Times have changed since his day.

Following his don's advice, my father sat the Indian Civil Service
exams. He passed them all, finishing in first place, so Grandpa's plans for
his business were not realized. Pa's younger brother, Arthur, stepped into
what could have been Pa's place in the company. Grandpa had been a phi-
lanthropist, building, for example, the Holly Lodge Estate, which is still
thriving, in Highgate, London. Here family apartments were intermingled with apartments for women who had been left widowed by the Great
War, each buying shares in the estate. My uncle built rows of small bungalows, "the slums of tomorrow" according to Pa. Later I remember hearing Pa say that while my uncle built bungalows, he himself proudly helped

My father as
a young man.

to build an empire. Grandpa, however, did not accept that building and maintaining an empire was more important than building buildings.

When Pa became a judge my grandmother realized that he would not be returning to the family business and asked Pa to send her a photograph of himself in his judge's wig and gown. It was not in Pa's nature to want to be photographed but she persisted until he finally relented. When my grandmother received the formal portrait she was so horrified that she immediately put it in her desk drawer out of sight. She could not accept that this was her son. Even his humorous touch of signing it "Judge Beetle Brows" did not endear her to this stranger in the photograph. The prodigal son would not be forgiven even though he had complied with her wishes on this occasion.

In order to be accepted for the Indian Civil Service Pa not only had to pass the very demanding examinations but he also had to learn fourteen Indian dialects as well as Urdu and Hindi, and he had to be able to write

Godfrey Davis, "Judge Beetle Brows."

My grandma Davis came from Manchester in the north of England. She sang in the Manchester choir and believed that what Manchester thought today London thought tomorrow. She insisted that her grownup children visit every week – although not my father because of being in India. When on leave, however, he always spent time with her. Grandma was upright, direct, and I remember when Anne and I had lunch with her we had green jelly. When I took a spoonful the vacuum caused by the removal of the spoon made a rude sound. No one remarked.

the historical language of Sanskrit. Ultimately he mastered twenty-two Indian dialects.

Pa became a member of the ICS in 1913. In his final interview he was asked whether he had any preference for his first posting. He replied that he would like to go where he was most needed. He sailed for India in 1914, arriving in Bombay where he worked for the secretariat in the Bombay Presidency.[4] Soon after, he was posted to Ahmedabad, in the province of Gujarat, as a magistrate. He was greatly appreciated there and dismayed when he was transferred almost immediately to another area where a terrible famine was raging. There had been a devastating drought, and the wealthy merchants were hoarding rice and selling it on the black market at exorbitant prices. The poor people, unable to meet the demands of the merchants, were dying of starvation. It was Pa's job to confiscate the rice from the merchants and ration it out so that everyone could have one good meal a day. The price had to be arranged so the merchants did not make great profits. There was so much corruption that Pa had to check continually that justice was being carried out. Even some of his underlings were being bribed by corrupt storekeepers, creating another problem for Pa. He was shocked by the starvation and it took time to get some semblance of aid in place for the victims. He felt as if he was living in biblical times. He had never seen such terrible sights nor expected to find such corruption. It must be remembered that he was only a young man fresh from the sheltered environment of Cambridge University.

One of Pa's colleagues, a young man who was rather spoiled and very hoity-toity, chose a plum job in Bangalore when he was asked where he would like to be posted. In this most beautiful province of southern India the temperate climate and lack of disease made for a very pleasant life, but this elegant young man did not enjoy it for very long. When the First World War broke out he was called up and killed tragically very early on. Pa sent in his papers to join up. He went for his interview but medically he was found unfit because of his flat feet: this was in the days when soldiers had to do a great deal of marching. My Uncle Herbert Ziman, however, a delicate man who was also thought unfit for military service, joined up as a war correspondent and got to the front lines on many occasions. When Pa insisted on being given work in the forces where his feet would not be a liability, he was informed that his work on famine duty was much too important. There was no one who could do the work as well as he, so he returned to where the earth was dry as dust and the seeds were shrunken. Water, which we so often take for granted, was non-existent. The heat was overpowering. The plight of the people was terrible but still no rain came. Pa had to be continually on the alert to find the merchants' secret hoards of rice, which he immediately confiscated.

———

Meanwhile in England my mother's older sister, Marie, became engaged to a New Zealand sheep farmer. Pa heard of Marie's engagement and panicked. He thought my mother would be next as arranged marriages were then an accepted form of love. He cabled my mother asking for her hand in marriage. He was not entitled to home leave for five years so my mother, if she accepted, would have to wait all that time before marrying. Happily she accepted and my parents kept their romance alive by writing long letters. Long-distance telephone calls had not yet been invented but in any case it would have been astronomically expensive to phone. Even as a child in the 1930s I don't think I ever spoke to my parents on the telephone.

India is known for the quality of its sapphires and Pa sent my mother a beautiful sapphire ring surrounded by tiny diamonds set in platinum. She was now truly engaged. After five years Pa returned to England. He married my mother in 1922, when she was twenty-seven and Pa was thirty-two, and they set sail for India. My mother was extremely brave to leave gentle England for India in the 1920s.

My mother, sylphlike in her wedding dress. She and Pa were engaged for five years, a long time to wait.

My parents' marriage had an eventful beginning. With all the farewells and last-minute packing they missed their train at Victoria Station and had to take a taxi all the way to Dover. This was a very expensive journey and my mother never forgot it because for the rest of his life Pa hated taxi rides. They made it in time to catch the ferry to Calais, which linked them with the boat train to Marseilles. The boat train from Calais to Marseilles was the first shock for my mother. The first-class sleeper bunks were covered in red velvet. During the day she sat on the lower berth in comparative comfort, although space was limited and they could not move around. In the evening the lower birth was pulled out to convert into a bed. The camouflage of red velvet was removed revealing a hard wooden bunk: not the sleeping arrangement a new bride hopes for on her honeymoon. In Marseilles they boarded the P&O liner that took them to India.

My mother's journey to India was coloured by one event. It was customary for the passengers to change every evening for dinner and this made dining a grand affair. It was terribly hot in the Suez Canal and my mother had to coax Pa to change into his stiff collar, bow tie, and dinner jacket. There were two bachelors on board who teased Pa for his lack of conformity. They were sharing a cabin on the port side and my mother and a young lady friend, Mary Perry, decided to pay them back for their criticism of Pa. They obtained the steward's permission to enter the bachelors' cabin and waited outside until they were sure the two men had left. Then, armed with a needle and thread, they went into the cabin. My mother found the bachelor's dinner jackets and sewed up the two left sleeves. Leaving no trace of themselves, they giggled their way back down the corridor.

After the bachelors, who later became my adopted uncles Streat and U'Ren, had their evening drink with Pa they went down to change. My mother and Mary Perry walked round the deck and stood outside the two men's cabin. They were not disappointed. It was extremely hot and loud curses and swearing flowed out of the porthole. Inside the two were performing acrobatics trying to get their arms into the left-hand sleeves,

Uncle Ben U'Ren of the Indian Police and his bride. En route to India, my mother and Mary Perry sewed up the sleeve of his dinner jacket.

pulling with their right hands to no avail. The sweat poured in a stream down their faces, wetting the front of their stiff shirts. These two other-wise intelligent men could not figure out why they could not release themselves from their contorted positions and dress in the usual way for their dinner. My mother and her friend could no longer smother their laughter and went wobbling down the deck like two drunks. In later years this prank was related many times and I found it amusing to see these four grey-haired distinguished-looking elders laughing anew at a much-retold memory.

Privacy at a Premium

My mother, as a young bride, experienced her first taste of India with Pa when he was stationed in Ahmedabad in the early 1920s. Pa had already been working in India for four years and loved it. For my mother there were many adjustments to be made.

She was the only white woman in Ahmedabad and she was embar-rassed by the way everyone stared at her. She was desperately homesick. My parents were befriended, however, by a lovely Indian family, the Am-balals. Papa Ambalal owned a large textile mill and my mother became very interested in weaving and learning the process of dyeing yarn. Mrs Ambalal invited my parents to dinner and with great tact showed my mother how to eat Indian food correctly. There was a fine wafer-thin cir-cular disc called a papadum that one did not bite directly but crunched in one's hands and crumbled over the rice and curry. It gave a delicious crispy taste to the soggy rice and vegetables. The Ambalals belonged to the Jain faith and Jains did not kill animals or harm insects. Despite cultural and political differences the Ambalals remained lifelong friends to my family.

One of the ways Mother found to fit into her new community was to join the local Red Cross, which held twice-weekly work parties. Throughout the day she was in touch with the servants who had been hired by Pa. They too had to adjust to having a memsahib in charge of the household. She must have been an exemplary employer as none of the servants left but stayed with our family for thirty years. My mother was now able to entertain and return the generous hospitality that Pa had received. In time the house became a real home.

A new country and new customs were not the only things my mother had to contend with. One evening she was having her much-enjoyed bath when a large black hairy hand undid the window latch, and an equally hairy long black arm slithered through the opening. My mother screamed and the hand and arm retreated, only to rapidly reappear. She threw her face cloth but the hand grabbed it. She realized then that the hand and arm belonged to a monkey, and the last thing she wanted was a monkey in her bathroom. The face cloth disappeared through the window but the monkey's hand reappeared as if wanting something more. My mother threw her favourite bar of Yardley's English lavender soap. To her amazement the monkey caught it and the soap also disappeared outside, but this time the monkey's hand did not reappear. Perhaps he had left to join his friends in the trees and share his booty. Would they eat the soap or use it for its rightful purpose? She really did not care but was disappointed to lose an irreplaceable souvenir from England. She speedily put the latch on the window, put on her bathrobe, and retreated to her bedroom to dress. What a scene met her eyes. The monkeys had invaded the sanctity of her bedroom. One was sitting on her dressing table admiring itself in the mirror and my mother expected that at any moment it would start powdering its nose and applying her lipstick. In desperation she threw her slipper, but the monkey caught it as if it was fielding a cricket ball and leaped out of the open window, taking the slipper with it. Two other monkeys were playing peek-a-boo with the covers on her bed. She aimed a heavier shoe at both of them, but one of the monkeys caught it and went bounding out of the window while the other waited hopefully for my mother to throw another shoe for it to catch. My mother wanted the monkey out before it made off with her pearl necklace, an heirloom. She sacrificed yet another shoe, hoping to frighten the monkey, but again the creature caught it and leapt happily through the open window with its booty. My mother shut the windows and lay exhausted on her bed, recovering from this new experience.

What would Godfrey say when she told him of the monkeys' lack of respect for her private bedroom? What if there had been a baby in the room? Would the monkeys have whisked it away? Rudyard Kipling would have had another tale to add to his *Jungle Book*. Would they return? Would she ever find her shoes again? How could she keep the monkeys out of her room? Suppose she and Godfrey set up a picnic table a safe distance from the house and her bedroom, laying it with food for a tea party as they did for the chimpanzees at the London Zoo?

Eventually my mother came to expect such adventures in India.

The monkeys outside my parents' house in Ahmedabad.

A Far Cry from London's Inner Temple

The life of a district magistrate was varied and unpredictable. When Pa was still a young junior magistrate he had to go on circuit and hold court in the outlying districts. He travelled by camel, slept in a tent, and enjoyed meeting the village people. Pa was deeply interested in agriculture and encouraged the villagers in their farming efforts. In one village he spoke with a wandering herdsman who led a nomadic life in order to find sufficient grazing for his sheep. Pa was so impressed with this proud handsome man that he discussed with him the idea of awarding a prize to the best ram in the local herds. The herdsman thought it a wonderful idea. Local men were selected as judges and a day was chosen for the contest. The event was publicized by word of mouth and Pa was invited to attend.

An arena was made and a stand erected from which Pa would perform the prize-giving. To his amazement, the first ram entered the arena followed by a great herd of sheep. The sheep, not used to being in a confined space, were soon milling about and pressing their powerful bodies against the stand where Pa sat. The judges were down among the sheep prodding and feeling the ram. Pa speedily joined them, fearing that the stand would collapse under the pressure of the herd jostling against it.

"Why," Pa asked in alarm, "are all the sheep necessary when it is the rams that are being judged?"

"The rams will not come unless they are followed by their flock," came the obvious reply.

The judging took the whole day. The villagers were delighted and the ram contest became an annual event. Over time it expanded to include goats, cows, and falcons. Unhappily, cockfights were also included and I am not sure whether Pa was able to humanize the rules. I know he felt there should have been enough excitement without bringing this cruel sport into an arena designed to encourage the improvement of local agriculture.

Pa on tour, riding his camel with an inappropriate saddle suitable only for carrying luggage: a big mistake.

Judging rams when Pa was on circuit in the rural areas.

Village life: a grandfather with his granddaughter and the precious family cow.

A handsome bull. Cows are sacred to the
Hindus and the cause of many court cases.
If a cow wandered onto Moslem territory
and was killed intentionally or not, there
would be a riot.

It was on one of his tours in a rural part of India that Pa, a lover of birds, was introduced to the black partridge. He had noticed an Indian peasant walking with a partridge cage balanced on his shoulder and a male partridge walking free on the ground behind him. The partridge cage consisted of two separate wicker cages suspended from a branch of wood that was balanced on the peasant's shoulders. Pa asked the partridge owner, "Are you not afraid that if your male partridge sees another female partridge he will scurry off?"

"Never," replied the shocked owner. "A partridge chooses his mate for life and will never leave her."

This owner had his female in one of the two cages he was carrying. When the male had had his exercise, he would put him in the empty wicker cage and allow the female out. Having the partridges in separate cages enabled him to walk freely, balancing the wicker containers on his shoulder.

On another tour Pa saw a local man weaving a partridge cage. Pa was so impressed with the man's skill that he asked if the weaver would teach him how to make the cages. It was arranged and the weaver came to the government circuit house, where Pa was staying. Thanks to his good teacher, Pa soon learned the new skill of weaving a partridge cage.

Of far less pleasure to my father than bird keeping and cage making were the duck shoots so popular with the zemindars, or landowners. As an ICS representative Pa received many invitations to duck shoots. He hated them but was obliged to accept at least one from every zemindar. The zemindars were my father's friends but love of duck shooting was not an emotion they shared. Were any extra ducks they shot given to the poor and hungry? No, my father was told. They were all eaten by the zemindar's household, which included his friends and his staff.

It was the beauty of the wild ducks in natural flight that my father loved. He did not enjoy watching the dogs flush them out or their trembling tumble from the sky as the guns were fired. No skill was needed by

Left: A friend showing a special carrying cage that could hold partridges in separate compartments.
Right: Pa learned from Indian peasants how to make different kinds of birdcages.

the hunters: the ducks were numerous and the dogs highly skilled, locating the fallen ducks and bringing them back to their masters.

The Indian assistants had to carry the zemindar and his guests through the muddy waters. The zemindar and the other hunters were not expected to get their clothes and feet wet and muddy.

At the close of the shoot the ducks were tied in pairs and laid in a line on the ground in front of each individual marksman in preparation for the great photograph taking. This was no small feat in the 1930s. The cumbersome, heavy camera equipment was not designed to be carried through swampy land.

My father's refusal actually to shoot ducks caused embarrassment to his host when it came to taking the photograph. He had no ducks to pose behind. To my father's amusement the problem was quickly resolved when the zemindar lay several brace of his own ducks at my father's feet.

My mother was never disappointed when my father returned from a duck shoot with no ducks. She did not find wild duck meat tasty. The cook was not disappointed either. He made a delicious vegetarian curry for my parents. He enjoyed their compliments and always made enough to take home to his wife and son.

Fortunately when my father retired in 1947 our cook also retired. He would have found it difficult to adjust to cooking for a family with more exacting tastebuds.

Wearing decoy ducks on their heads, Indian duck hunters would go underwater and pull unsuspecting ducks under by their feet.

Egrets and herons with their throats tied so they can't swallow the fish they catch, which are then collected by the fishermen.

Court sessions were normally very serious and in at least one case proved deadly. In 1930 justice was being made a mockery of in the court of Karachi, Sind, which is now Pakistan. Pa, sent to rectify the situation, had a taste of what was going on soon after his appointment. He received threatening letters: his two daughters, Joyce baba and Wendy baba, a seven-year-old and a two-year-old, would be kidnapped if the judge made the wrong decision. Extra protection for his family and household was provided. My Pa was determined to uphold the legal system. This did not prevent one litigant from taking justice into his own hands. One day Pa was hearing a case when, unnoticed by anyone in the courtroom, two men moved stealthily forward, row by row, until they were seated behind one of the witnesses. They pulled him over the back of the seat, stabbed him dead, then made their escape in the resulting hubbub.

Pa was horrified at the murder and at the insult to him and to the justice system. It did not prevent him from improving the administration of

Pa and my mother with law students in Gujarat. In those days in India, if a student failed an exam, he believed that it was to his credit to say that he had attempted the exam, no matter how many times, as he had gained knowledge with each try.

justice. But it took many years of hard work and writing judgments late into the night. The improvements in the system were recognized by the viceroy, Lord Linlithgow, who honoured Pa in 1940 by upgrading his court in Karachi to a high court and naming him chief judge. Indian law students came from far and wide to sit in on Pa's court sessions. They claimed that they learned more from attending his cases than they did from their lectures and books.

Law students, Ahmedabad, Gujarat, ca. 1920. Pa is seated ninth from the right in the second row.

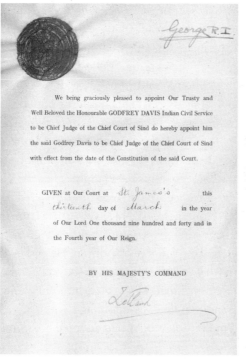

We being graciously pleased to appoint Our Trusty and Well Beloved the Honourable GODFREY DAVIS Indian Civil Service to be Chief Judge of the Chief Court of Sind do hereby appoint him the said Godfrey Davis to be Chief Judge of the Chief Court of Sind with effect from the date of the Constitution of the said Court.

GIVEN at Our Court at *St. James's* this *thirteenth* day of *March* in the year of Our Lord One thousand nine hundred and forty and in the Fourth year of Our Reign.

BY HIS MAJESTY'S COMMAND

Pa becomes chief judge of the high court in Sind, 1940.

Gandhi

Gandhi was born in Porbandar in the state of Gujarat. Ambalal befriended Gandhi and gave him a gift of land in Ahmedabad, where Gandhi
built his ashram. During the 1920s Pa was also in Ahmedabad with the
Indian Civil Service. Indeed, Pa's time in India, 1914–47, coincided with
Gandhi's: Gandhi returned to India after his years in South Africa in 1915
and was assassinated in 1948. It was a chaotic and violent time during
which Britain's empire disintegrated and those who worked for the ICS
presided over the dismantling or transfer of their jobs.

The mass agitations instigated by Gandhi against British rule brought
him into Pa's orbit. They became friends, a friendship that brought both
pleasure and grief. While Pa essentially agreed with Gandhi, he believed
that the Indian people had to be trained to accept democratic principles before gaining their independence. It was Pa's duty to control the chaos that
Gandhi was causing as he incited people to acts to civil disobedience. In
one such campaign, the economy of Gujarat was held to ransom for four
weeks as all workers in the textile mills, including those owned by Ambalal, left their looms and staged a strike. Gandhi supported the workers
and began to fast; after three days the mill owners agreed to arbitration.

In 1921 Gandhi became leader of the Indian National Congress, which
declared its faith in civil disobedience. After an Indian mob set fire to a
police station, killing the constables inside, Gandhi called off a mass non-
violent campaign planned for February 1922 and undertook a fast as
penance for the violence. Nonetheless, Pa received orders from the viceroy
to stop Gandhi's destructive behaviour and imprison him. Gandhi was
duly arrested in Ahmedabad on a charge of sedition. He was given his only
judicial trial on 10 March 1922 and sentenced to six years, to be served at
the Yeravada prison in Ahmedabad.[5] Pa visited him daily and they had
long discussions about India. Like Pa, Gandhi as a young man had studied at the Inns of Court in London, but he had adopted the spinning wheel

as his symbol, representing the peasants who were the majority of the Indian population. In the course of their conversations Gandhi suggested that the prisoners should learn a trade and that it should be weaving. Pa enthusiastically followed through with this idea.

So it was that the prisoners became weavers, creating heavy cotton shirts. To make the weaving more interesting a red stripe was woven into the cloth. Unfortunately when the shirts were washed the red stripe ran. Of course Pa purchased the shirts to wear. My mother was horrified when she saw him wearing a bloody-looking shirt that made him look like a butcher. Pa refused to take it off. My mother, with incredible fore-sight, arranged with our head bearer, Fernandes, to purchase more shirts from the prison. Every time the shirts needed washing she substituted a new shirt for the old one. Fernandes suggested that the dirty shirts should be washed and given to the servants, who would wear them as under-shirts. Pa and the governor of the prison were delighted with the increase in sales. Gandhi and the prisoners were delighted that their enterprise was so successful.

One day while Pa was talking to Fernandes he noticed red stripes showing through his crisp white outer shirt. "Oh good, you are wearing one of the shirts made by the prisoners." Fernandes without hesitation replied, "Yes, Sahib, the rough cotton feels good against my skin and ab-sorbs my sweat." Pa was unaware both of Fernandes's embarrassment and his conspiracy with my mother.

Gandhi was often imprisoned on other occasions during Pa's spell of duty and fasted near to death.[6] Pa always visited him and saw that he had every comfort possible. Pa told me many stories of Gandhi, whom he loved and respected. Gandhi's many admirers stayed at his ashram and those from England and Europe often followed their stay with a visit to my parents. Our cook was puzzled that all these visitors craved omelettes filled with finely chopped spring onions. He mentioned the fact to Pa who was equally puzzled but determined to solve this mystery. One of Gandhi's admirers, a lady called Mirabehn who came from a well-respected family in England, was one of my parents' guests.[7] She had a lovely English rose complexion but otherwise, according to Pa, was rather mousey and quiet. Pa took her into his confidence and asked, "Why do you and all other visitors who come from Gandhi's ashram want an omelette with a filling of finely chopped spring onions for breakfast?"

Mirabehn looked away from Pa and asked, "Do I have to respond to your question?" Pa replied, "It is my cook who has brought this demand for omelettes to my notice and he wonders if Gandhi's cook would like a lesson on how to make an omelette with spring onions." Mirabehn replied, "Oh no, Gandhi's cook knows how to cook omelettes with onions. It is Gandhi himself who will not allow his cook to provide a meal with eggs and onions. He believes," Mirabehn continued, blushing slightly, "that *eggs and onions cooked together, when eaten, excite the passions.*"

Pa, not wanting to embarrass Mirabehn, suppressed the laughter that threatened to burst forth and responded in accordance with her demure behaviour. He found it extraordinary to think that Gandhi was concerned that Mirabehn might show passion as she was so well brought up and so shy. The mystery of the omelette with chopped spring onions was now solved, but how was Pa to explain it to our cook respectfully and without laughing?

Gandhi was also a great believer in the use of garlic. All our visitors who came to stay after visiting his ashram smelled strongly of garlic. He believed that garlic was a preventative and a cure for many ailments. He educated my Pa, who had previously disliked garlic, to the extent that years later, in retirement in England, Pa applied garlic to the beaks of his most beloved golden pheasants when they developed severe colds: no easy task as it involved my holding the pheasants while Pa rubbed their beaks with the garlic clove. Miraculously they recovered. Pa wished that Gandhi had written a cookbook for it would have been very interesting.

During one of Pa's visits to the ashram Gandhi opened his desk drawer and pulled out a picture of Jesus, saying, "Do you not think He has a beautiful face, Godfrey?" As Pa looked at the picture Gandhi continued: "In order to be beautiful I believe it is necessary to suffer."

Gandhi was continually organizing peaceful processions and marches. In 1930 he organized the famous Salt March to protest the British tax on salt and monopoly on salt production. He led seventy-eight members of his ashram on a twenty-four-day four-hundred-kilometre march from Ahmedabad to the sea at Dandi. There he picked up a handful of salt on the shore. This single act set in motion a train of events that saw people along India's coastline collecting salt and selling it tax free. In Ahmedabad ten thousand people obtained illegal salt from the Indian Congress in the first week after Gandhi picked up the salt at Dandi. Thousands were arrested and imprisoned including Gandhi, who wrote to Mirabehn a week after his imprisonment, "I have been quite happy in making up arrears in sleep."

Once when Pa was in England he received a telephone call from Gandhi.[8] He and his colleagues were staying at Toynbee Hall in the East End of London and Gandhi wanted Pa to meet them at the entrance to the Poplar Tube Station at approximately ten o'clock that morning. Pa willingly and hurriedly took the tube to Poplar and waited patiently for Gandhi and his entourage to arrive. Gandhi wore his Indian clothes with no overcoat despite the cold of the September day, and his wife wore a beautiful sari. With them were the shy faithful Mirabehn and several other followers. They wanted to visit the Houses of Parliament and set off in the Underground for Westminster. Pa felt slightly embarrassed as they all went down the escalator to the train. At that time few in England had seen people of

A shrine to Ghandi at the ashram at Sabarmati. Written in Gujarati above his picture: "In memory of Gandhi's fight for Indian independence." Gandhi believed that an evil thought was the same as an act of violence.

any nationality other than their white neighbours. Pa prayed fervently that his guests would not clear their throats and spit heartily, as they would habitually do in India. Gandhi and his male colleagues chewed betel nut, which turns the saliva a bright red colour and, when spat out, stains the pavement. While this habit was to Pa and his Indian friends less objectionable than smoking cigarettes, it was bound to be less acceptable to the British public. Pa was also afraid that Mrs Gandhi would trip on her sari as she stepped off the escalator.

Explaining himself to Gandhi, he stepped ahead of her so that he could help her alight from the moving stairs. They all had a wonderful day but none of the party wanted to eat at lunchtime; instead they insisted on sightseeing until three in the afternoon. Pa came home exhausted and famished.

Two

❦

Between Two Worlds

Adventures of Our Ayah

In those days most British mothers in India went to England to give birth and returned to India with their infants. My sister, Joyce, was born five years before I was and, once back in India, my mother had an ayah to look after her during her early years. I was born in 1928 and my mother then took me to India by sea. It must have been difficult for my sister now that Ayah had me to care for as well. With my parents' agreement she was also bringing up a friend's son, Lewis. My sister was reluctant to eat her food at mealtimes and Lewis unwittingly came to Ayah's rescue. He would stand on his head for fun and this made Joyce laugh. The moment her mouth was open in popped a spoonful of food that Ayah had in readiness.

Baby Joyce and our mother
before returning to India.

Ayah was very protective of her extended English family. Trains in India had ladies-only compartments and ladies had separate sleeping compartments from the men. On one train journey my mother, who was sleeping in the bottom bunk, was awakened by a loud thump. The train had stopped at a station and the door had been opened by one of the many male travellers looking for a carriage to sit in. Ayah, from the top bunk, had hit the unsuspecting traveller over the head with her shoe, saying, "You are not going to touch my Memsahib." Stunned, the interloper reeled backwards onto the platform into the darkness. My mother was horrified and, knowing Ayah's strength, afraid the man might be concussed. Ayah, however, remained unrepentant, believing that she was only doing her duty.

When Pa's leave came due in 1933, naturally Ayah came to England with us. Our cook's wife offered to care for Lewis. She and her husband were going to their home state of Goa so they would all have a change of scene and be with other members of their own family.

In England my parents had booked a holiday in Bude, Cornwall, in a small family-style hotel. One morning one of the guests entered the dining room in a slight state of alarm. He had seen a strange person sitting on the

Ayah holding my hand at our house in Highgate, London.

roof smoking a large pipe. The person had a garment wrapped round his or her head that looked decidedly like someone's Chilprufe long under-wear. My parents gasped. They realized that it must be our ayah. She loved to smoke her hookah (a waterpipe for smoking tobacco) but my parents had tried to dissuade her as there was nowhere appropriate for her to smoke it. She had cleverly found the flat roof where no one would be annoyed by her smoking. The guest was correct about the underwear. Pa also felt the cold. He had mislaid one pair of his long underwear but until now had thought nothing of it.

My parents had to persuade the hotel proprietor that Ayah could offi-cially have her morning smoke on the hotel's flat roof. The management had never had such a request, but after checking with their insurance pol-icy and obtaining a signed document from Pa stating that he would be re-sponsible for any consequences resulting from Ayah's smoking habits, all was well. The guests had been alerted and were amenable to our ayah's solution to her dilemma of adapting to a different country.

One of my most endearing memories of Ayah in England was the way she prepared me for sleep. She lit the gas fire and hung my pyjamas over the rail on the fireguard and warmed a small green square bottle of cam-phorated oil in a small jug of hot water. After having fun in the bath and being thoroughly dried, I snuggled in front of the fire wrapped in a warm towel. In the darkened room I watched fascinated as the gas flames flick-ered among the bars, sometimes red, sometimes yellow, sometimes blue, a wonderful fantasy of colour. Then there was the smell of the warm oil. Ayah lowered the towel to my waist and, dipping her long fingers into the camphorated oil, massaged it into my back and chest with firm but gentle hands. My body tingled. The rest of the room was freezing cold but this was our little imaginary India. Then I dressed in my warmed pyjamas. I was allowed to enjoy the colours of the gas fire before saying my brief prayer – "Thank you God for a lovely day. Amen." Sliding between the cold bedsheets, the warmth of the camphorated oil worked pleasantly through my body as I fell asleep.

Nowadays it is when I wake up that I think nostalgically of our ayah. I imagine her massaging my miserable knees with warm camphorated oil and amazingly they seem less painful and more mobile.

As the time for our return to India approached Ayah decided that she should buy a new suitcase. The one she showed my parents was of a far superior quality to anything they owned. Pa complimented her on her choice of luggage and asked her where she had bought it. "Harrods," she replied. "Harrods?" Pa hesitantly responded. We lived in Highgate, North London, and Harrods was in South Kensington, a considerable distance by bus and Underground. Pa was amazed at Ayah's independence, travelling all that way. "There is a good luggage shop in Camden Town; why go all the way to South Kensington?" Pa enquired. "Harrods is special and I have heard others talk about shopping there and I wanted to see for myself." Good for Ayah, Pa thought, and tactfully continued. "But Ayah, how much did it cost?" To which Ayah replied, "Nothing." "Nothing?" Pa was amazed. He never thought for one minute that she had stolen it but perhaps she had put it on my mother's account. While these thoughts were passing through his mind, Ayah said in all seriousness, "I created a scene. I stood on a chair and rubbed my stomach and said my master starved me. A few people gathered round and then a very smart man in a well-cut suit came and helped me down from the chair I had been standing on. He said I could keep the suitcase and escorted me to the large revolving doors at the entrance. I could not get in the revolving doors with my suitcase so he opened another exit door for me. I caught the bus and put the suitcase in the space for luggage. I sat on a seat opposite in case anyone took it. Now it is safely home and I can pack it when we all return to India."

A Policeman's Lot Can Be a Happy One

When Pa drove his car in Karachi the policemen recognized him and waved him on. There were few cars at the time and no traffic lights, and drivers had to share the road with bicycles, donkey carts, tongas (horse-drawn carriages) and camel carts. When he was on leave in England he only had to share the road with other cars but no one gave him the respect he received in Karachi. This did not prevent him from having some amusing encounters with the British bobby. Traffic lights were minimal at the time and it was mainly the police who directed the traffic.

On one occasion when Pa was driving cautiously, he was surprised to be stopped by a policeman.

"Do you realize you are driving down a one-way street the wrong way?" the policeman demanded.

Laughing, Pa replied, "I wondered why the traffic was going the wrong way." The policeman fortunately had a sense of humour and did not ticket Pa. Another time my mother insisted on buying a delectable but smelly cheese. Pa was equally insistent that she hold it out of the car window on the way home. At the end of the road where a policeman was directing traffic, Pa put his hand out to go left. The policeman was completely baffled because my mother in the passenger seat was holding the smelly cheese out of the window, indicating to the policeman that they were turning right. The policeman cautioned my parents to stop their car and asked which way they were going. Pa, feeling guilty about asking my mother to hold the cheese out of the window, explained with a touch of laughter that they could not decide. Again, the policeman was good-humoured and waited for them to decide; and again, they were fortunate not to be given a fine.

Anne before going to India in 1940.

Anne

One night at the end of Pa's 1933 leave, my parents introduced me to Anne Ayres. I had met Anne on various occasions but now, my mother explained, Anne was to be my constant companion. My mother, Pa, and Ayah were to return to India and Joyce and I were to stay in England. They were leaving in the morning but they would write to us and Anne would love me and take care of me. In return I must be kind and helpful to her. I was five and it would be another five years before I saw my parents again.

I remember waking up the next morning to the sunshine streaming through the window. This was very different to my usual awakening as Ayah always kept the curtains closed and I dressed by the light of the reading lamp. Then I remembered what my parents had told me the night before. Anne was looking after me now.

Anne had beautiful reddish golden hair which she wore in braids around her head. She had a gentle voice, white freckled skin, and a friendly smile. She was an orphan and at eighteen years of age had been the under-nanny with friends of my parents'. Now she had the responsibility of taking my parents' place and bringing me up. She had to liaise between my sister, me, and my parents.

That day, she explained, we were going on an adventure, not to India but to Angmering-on-Sea where I would be going to a boarding school. I had no idea what that meant but I knew that my older sister was already at a boarding school. Our adventure involved taking a train from Victoria Station to Sussex with my beloved rabbit, Cottontail, Paddy our spaniel, and Edward and Jubilee, our tortoises. Our budgerigars would stay behind in our London house. A married couple, Mr and Mrs Baines, would be living in the house and caring for our birds. We would return to London with my sister for the school holidays.

I did not realize how fortunate we were to have Anne. She was my companion, sharing a room with me at Willowhayne School. I did not have to spend holidays moving from one relative to another like so many of my friends whose fathers worked in foreign countries. I also had the continuity of returning to our house in Highgate with our aviary of budgerigars.

Meanwhile, Anne kept in touch with my parents by weekly letters. While I was at Willowhayne School I never remember Anne having any days off to be with her friends, June and Eileen Ferrier. She must have had time to herself while I was at classes but at all other times she was there with me. We went for walks together and grew a small garden where I

Anne looking after me at Angmering-on-Sea, Sussex.
Holding Anne's hand was always comforting to me.

planted seeds and learned the wonders of nature. Indeed, Anne was responsible for many of the pupils having tiny plots in which they could
grow plants from seed. Anne taught me to knit and embroider and in the
winter I learned to skate on Patcham Pond. We went for outings to the tea-
house at Hercemoncieux, we walked on the Downs, and we visited my sister at Roedean School in Brighton.

At Christmas we returned to 4 Robin Grove, Highgate, where my sister joined us for her school holidays. We received exciting presents from my parents, wonderful gifts from India: fluffy white cottonballs grown on bushes; lovely silk scarves and Indian dolls wearing saris; sandalwood letter openers – all mysterious and deliciously scented.

When my parents finally returned, we went to Victoria Station to meet them. The station was frighteningly crowded. Suddenly we were immersed in smoke as the steam train arrived. The cloud of steam lifted and Anne recognized my parents. She told me to run up and hug them but I held even harder to her hand. I refused to go and hug these strangers walking toward me. My parents understood and my mother gently lifted me up and kissed me on the forehead. She passed me to my father who ruffled my hair and gave me back to the security of Anne. My father wore a Harris tweed jacket with a comforting scent that I have always associated with him.

When the family returned to India Anne went with us. She had many beaux but she never married. My mother always hoped that Anne would have her own family and home; it was hard to live constantly with other people's families.

When I was old enough to go to boarding school alone Anne went to another family, the Mallens. When their children went to boarding school Anne came back to us for a while before going to our neighbours in Kent, Lady Felicity Longmore and her family. Lady Felicity was the daughter of Lord Wavell, viceroy of India from 1943 to 1947. The Longmores valued Anne greatly.

Anne stayed with the Longmore family until she retired. They found her a ground-floor flat with a garden in Chichester, near to where they were living. After I moved to Canada, Andrew Longmore, Lady Felicity's son, enabled me to visit Anne on my holidays in Edinburgh, Scotland. I would fly down to Gatwick where Andrew would meet me and drive me

Anne led me astray. A glass of ginger beer, which I was not allowed to drink inside, was my reward afer skating on Patcham Pond in Sussex.

Below: Grandma Ziman accompanying me on a ride in Sussex. David Ziman invested heavily in a mine that, at the time, failed to produce, though it later became profitable. When he died at fifty-eight, Grannie was left quite hard up with three children to educate.

Anne with Joyce and me at the Sussex coast.

to Anne's flat. We always had fun on these visits. Thankfully, Andrew always kept in touch with me.

Anne died after a short illness, at the age of ninety-five, much loved by all her families.

———

Growing up in England before the Second World War and only seeing Pa every five years, he was always a stranger when he arrived. But on one of his leaves he quickly built up our friendship by asking me to help him make cages for his canaries. I was naturally thrilled. We would take the trolley at Parliament Hill Fields and change to a bus at Kentish Town, finally alighting at Camden Town near Pa's favourite hardware shop. I loved the smell of the wood and the vibrant atmosphere as everyone selected the materials they needed for their special creations. We would buy a roll of wire and pieces of wood to make the frames of the cages, also pieces of zinc to make the trays. On one return journey as we were boarding the bus a workman said to Pa, "I'm luckier than you, mate, I'm going off duty now." Pa gave him a great smile and was delighted to be taken for a skilled carpenter. At the final part of the journey we hiked up Highgate Hill, no mean feat with our purchases, but soon we were home at 4 Robin Grove.

The next day I helped Pa straighten the wire. In the garden nearest the house he had placed a post in the ground. In the post there was a wrought iron ring to which we attached one end of the wire. Then at the far end of the garden he had another piece of wood with a wrought iron ring. To this ring he attached the end of the wire that he had cut from the coil. This piece of wood he angled so the base rested on the ground and then with great strength he tried to make the top of the wood vertical to the base, thus extending and straightening the wire. He pulled once, twice, and yet a third time, becoming redder in the face with each pull. The wire was now straight and he could work with it. Another length of wire was cut and the straightening procedure repeated. This time it was my turn. Pa assured me it needed more strength than I could provide, but I insisted on trying. I pulled but instead of my straightening the wire it hurtled me into the air and I came falling down while the wire retained its original coil.

When sufficient lengths of wire had been straightened and cut Pa drilled equidistant holes in a piece of wood. I was amazed by the way the drill burrowed into the wood, making a perfect hole and ejecting delightful squiggly pieces of wood shavings. I saved these shavings because I had great plans to make a Father Christmas and use them for his beard. It was my job to thread a length of wire into the holes drilled in the wood that formed the top, bottom, and sides of the cage. An opening had to be made large enough to get one's hand into the cage and this necessitated making a special wire attachment that slid up and down. Two more openings had to be made for the food and water containers. A further opening was made at the top of the cage for a nesting box to use in the breeding season. The cage had to have a divider so that a sick or aggressive bird could be segregated.

Pa experimented with the width, length, and depth of the cage. He endeavoured to make small, manageable cages that were still large enough to give his canaries sufficient space to exercise their wings. A great deal of work and pride went into making a birdcage. Pa naturally never wanted to part with a single one. On returning to India from one of their leaves, my parents planned to rent our house in London. Durtnells, the storage company, stored three hundred birdcages. My mother never flinched when she received the bill.

Pa and me, with our dog Bunty, in Karachi.

When I was at school in England, I was asked by my teacher what Pa did in India. I said he made birdcages. There was an intense silence. This was not the response she wanted. She had evidently planned her whole lesson on the builders of the British Empire, from the days of Queen Victoria to the present. Unknown to me she had specialized in the East India Company. And here in her class was a daughter of one of the knights of the empire who referred to her father as a birdcage maker. At the time I had no idea what disappointment I had caused my teacher.

A Brief Home Leave

My mother had arranged a holiday for us all when she and Pa returned to England in 1938. We were to stay on a farm, Little Bullhornstone, in South Brent, Devon.

Our holiday began with a train ride from Victoria Station to South Brent. From South Brent we had to take a taxi to get to Little Bullhornstone. The taxi was owned by Leslie Hard who became a good friend, and later on during the war he met up with us again in Karachi where he was serving with the Royal Air Force.

My mother had not been to visit Little Bullhornstone but she had been writing to Mrs French, the farmer's wife, who was very encouraging of our visit. When Leslie drove us to the farm we were all pleasantly surprised. We congratulated Mother for having found a perfect summer place for us. The view from the stone house looked on to a tor, a small mountain. There were no other houses visible and the greenness of the countryside made a welcome change for my parents from the arid Sind desert.

There were two houses on the farm, the one occupied by Mr and Mrs French, and, six miles up the lane, the original farmhouse where Mr French's brother lived with his wife and family. The Frenches' two sons,

John and Jeffrey, lived with their uncle and his family in the original farmhouse while we stayed at their house. The farm was remote, with no bus
service, but they lent us their bicycles. The countryside was hilly and the
lanes narrow but there was little traffic so we envisaged good cycling. In
front of a hedgerow by our new home was a small natural pond where the
ducks amused themselves and provided endless entertainment. This was
before television; the wireless was all we needed. Best of all, the Frenches
had three riding ponies, Rufus, Bracken, and Starlight.

On our first morning John French was booked to take my father, my
sister, and myself for a ride on the moors. We were to be ready at 8:30 A.M.
and we would be away for two hours only as John had important duties
on the farm. When John arrived with the ponies, we mounted and set off
immediately onto the moors. My sister, being a teenager, found John at-
tractive and they led the way, chatting happily. My father, as always, was
deep in thought so I made friends with Rufus, my pony. The moors
shrouded in morning mist were creepy and made more so by the fact that
we kept losing sight of each other. Finally the mist lifted and we were
bathed in warm sunshine. We all loved being in the countryside with its
sights and sounds so different from London, where the traffic made a con-
tinuous rumble. We were stiff the next day but this did not deter us from
going for exploratory rides on the moors. Either John or Jeffrey would
take us for a long ride on Dartmoor every day.

We wasted no time in entering the life of the farm. We were welcome
to share in the farming activities: feeding the pigs, finding the eggs layed
by what are now termed "free range" chickens, feeding the ducks, helping
to bottle-feed a baby lamb, and helping to bring in the harvest. We also
learned how to hand milk the cows.

After a week of bliss the Frenches invited us into their kitchen to listen
to the news on their radio. Everyone was silent, filled with a sense of fore-
boding. Mr Chamberlain had returned from Germany with a peace treaty
signed by Hitler.[9] War had been averted. This did not stop the Indian Civil

Pa and Wendy during an early-morning ride on Dartmoor with John French.

Service from sending Pa a telegram informing him that he must return to India immediately. Immediate it was and the next morning we said our goodbyes to Pa, but at least my mother was staying with us. Pa had not been home for five years; after a week of getting to know him he was gone. He had become a good friend.

Pa sailed from Liverpool and wrote us brief letters. He told us later that he was on an overcrowded troopship. The captain was short of crew; he asked for volunteers to form a committee and help him with the everyday running of the ship. My father immediately responded. At first he thought what a tragedy it would be if the ship was torpedoed with all these intelligent men serving India on board, but after a week he changed his mind. The captain wanted volunteers to fold and secure deckchairs every night so that they wouldn't go overboard in a rough sea. No one volunteered. Then the passengers began to complain. One passenger was annoyed because the rice pudding was made without an egg. Shocked, my father replied that we were not living in the time of Mrs Beeton's cookbook – soon all food would be in short supply. Other passengers walked around with two glasses for their beer; as they explained, "If we put our empty glass down we might have to wait for it to be washed before we can get another drink."

I had made my father a grey sleeveless cablestitch pullover. I had knitted the heavy wool on thick needles as it was easier and quicker to make than a fine stocking-stitch sweater. Pa wore it like a uniform every day but always over a clean shirt. He did not know that the passengers were betting he would take his pullover off when the ship went through the intense heat of the Suez Canal and the Red Sea. My father never did stop wearing his sleeveless pullover and all the passengers lost their bets. When he was informed of this later, he claimed that many of the passengers drank too much, were overheated, and sweated profusely. He suggested that they encourage their daughters to knit them sleeveless pullovers, which would help them maintain an even body temperature.

Apocryphal or not, my father related the following anecdote: a sailor was scrubbing the deck when a passenger needed a lavatory in a hurry as he was feeling seasick. He asked the sailor for directions. The sailor politely responded, "Take a right, then a left and go down three stairs where you will see a sign saying GENTLEMEN." The sailor continued, "Don't let that deter you."

My father's ship arrived safely without incident in the port of Bombay, thanks to a brave captain and a wonderful crew.

The Days of the Cables

It was in September 1940 that the cables came. My mother, Anne, and I were still living in South Brent in a rented house. I went to Totnes County School while Joyce was at school in Brighton, on the south coast. South Brent had only a small post office with one employee. When the postmaster had to deliver a cable by bicycle the post office had to be closed. Each cable upset my mother more that the last. What were these cables, I wondered? My mother seemed all absorbed by them. She talked to Anne, and Anne listened. Why were we getting so many cables? Why was my mother so secretive about them? They were like gunfire attacking the house, causing chaos so that nothing went smoothly. Even our dog, Paddy, had gone berserk. When I saw him leaping and jumping on top of another dog that seemed to be cowering beneath him, I ran to my mother in great distress. She curtly dismissed me, making no attempt to increase my woefully inadequate sexual knowledge.

One morning at breakfast my mother burst into tears. I had never seen her cry. I was no longer a baby and I wanted to be included in this trouble that had been caused by the arrival of yet another cable. But it was not until a decision was reached that I learned what had caused my mother so much distress. The first cable from Pa in India read, *Leave Britain immediately. Take the children to your sister Marie in New Zealand. Please cable me that you have followed my plans. Godfrey.*

The next day, before we had even started breakfast, another cable arrived. It read, *Use your own intuition. I am not there to know the situation. Joyce's schooling must not be disturbed until she has completed her matriculation. Godfrey.*

Joyce, meanwhile, wrote to my mother that she was nearer to the Germans than she was to us. This was true: Brighton was closer than any other part of England to France and the Channel Islands, now occupied by the Germans. Illuminated by the famous white cliffs of Dover, Brighton was only a hop, skip, and a jump away.

During this time Anne had fallen off her bicycle in one of the hilly lanes and broken her hip. She had to be taken to the nearest hospital, which was in Plymouth, the seaport in Devon. Plymouth had been flattened by German bombers and we were scared that Anne would be killed whilst in hospital by a bomb. The Germans had no respect for hospitals.

Then there was my maternal grandmother, Lena Ziman, now wid-owed and living in a boarding house in London. Grandmother Davis's house had already been flattened, fortunately while she and her compan-ion were not at home. She was now living in an apartment close to her married children and grandchildren. Hitler's blitzkrieg was blasting Lon-don. This was no place to leave Grandmother Ziman, so more cables came and were left unopened while my mother went to London to fetch her mother. My mother had found a lovely lady in the village who was happy to cook and care for my grandmother, but Grandmother did not want to leave her home. My mother took her in a taxi and showed her all the flattened houses, including my other grandmother's house, and the de-struction caused by the German bombing raids in London. My grand-mother finally agreed and my mother brought her safely to South Brent. Grandmother was a Londoner; the green fields and munching cows did not please her. In London she enjoyed watching the trains from her sitting room, the noise and bustle of the people. Like the schoolchildren evacu-ated from London, she could not stand "the bloody hush of the country-side." My mother was satisfied however, that she had done the right thing. We could visit Grandmother daily.

My sister's persuasive letters from Roedean School, Brighton, did not sway my mother: Joyce had to take her matriculation. But this did not stop my mother from booking our passages to India.

Another cable came from Pa. *Use your own discretion. A convoy of school children on the Atlantic en route to North America has been torpe-doed. Affectionately Godfrey.*

My mother was helped in her decision by the Indian Civil Service, which allocated ships to bring the children of parents serving in India out to join them. The government's conclusion was that every mouth out of Britain was one less to feed. Rationing had already begun in Great Britain and food would become even scarcer as the war continued. My mother made her decision.

She would not go directly to New Zealand but would travel on one of the ships going to India. After visiting with Pa we would continue on to New Zealand. We said goodbye to our friends and to Paddy, our springer spaniel, Cottontail, our pet rabbit, Edward and Jubilee, our tortoises, our dolls, teddy bears, rocking-horse, and our rented house. Fortunately we did not have to say goodbye to Anne, who was returning to India with us.

Now we were on our way to see my father, chugging along in a train to Liverpool. With the help of Thomas Cook Travel Agents our mother had booked two rooms in a small family hotel. We reached Liverpool before dark and took a taxi to the hotel, the Lord Nelson. After helping to unload our luggage, the friendly taxi driver left us. There was nothing very familial about the hotel. An Indian was pacing our corridor. He had wavy black Brylcreemed hair and wore white flannel trousers and a white blazer, which looked strange in this dark, dank hotel. He was not my image of the picturesque Indian wearing a brilliantly coloured turban. We walked down the stairs to the dining area where we were to have high tea. A tired waitress showed us to a table. It held a tiered stand with dried-up sandwiches and even dryer pieces of cake on which a dead fly reposed. Did it die from eating a morsel of cake? We were about to depart when the waitress returned with boiled eggs. This was a miracle in wartime. Cartons of bought eggs often contained old eggs mixed in with fresh; when cooking with eggs we cracked them individually into a cup in case one was bad and would spoil a fresh egg. Fortunately our boiled eggs were good and a cup of tea brought some pleasure to the meal. However, we left as soon as we were finished.

We had been given one bedroom in which there were two double beds. Our mother pulled back the sheets to discover that they were dirty. But it was wartime; we did not think that we should complain. I speedily changed into my new aertex pyjamas. They had been bought two sizes too large so that I could grow into them, but this made walking difficult. I made it down the corridor to the lavatory but when I pulled the toilet chain the whole water cistern emptied down on me. I burst into tears, which ran down into my already soaked pyjamas. I managed to get back to the bedroom where Anne quickly dried me and put me into a second pair of equally large pyjamas. I wanted to hide in the cupboard but alas, I could not open it. There was a large hook on the outside of the door that reminded me of Peter Pan's Captain Hook, which reduced me to further tears.

My mother decided that we had to leave the hotel. My sister telephoned a young army officer, Guy Forte, whom she had met on the train. He was staying at the Adelphi, the most expensive hotel in Liverpool. He fetched us in a taxi and took us to his hotel where the only accommodation was the bridal suite. I remember entering the hotel with a blanket around my shoulders, tripping over my pyjama legs and finding myself in a brightly lit ballroom full of dazzling men and women dancing to an orchestra in full swing. The women wore long, elegant dresses and were partnered by soldiers in army uniform. I believe they thought we had been bombed out of our home but thankfully they kept on dancing. We took the elevator to the top floor of the hotel and were soon ensconced in the luxury of the bridal suite. We had just settled down for the night when the air-raid siren began to wail. The electricity was turned off so we had to walk down ten flights of stairs at least to the air-raid shelter in the basement of the hotel. We found a space to settle down and then the "all clear" sounded. Up the stairs we trudged. No sooner had we reached our room, it seemed, than the siren sounded again and down the stairs we went. My mother decided, as did many other mothers, that we would spend the night in the shelter and get some sleep.

The next morning we hurriedly packed and took a taxi to the docks where we were to board our ship, the *SS Orion*, a P&O liner, for India. My gas mask hung from my shoulder in a green canvas case. Just before boarding the ship an official said, "You won't need that where you are going but someone else can use it so it will stay here." As I climbed the ship's boarding ramp I felt as though I was leaving a part of me behind. The mask had been my constant companion, like my school satchel.

The ship filled me with pleasure. I soon made friends with others my age but my sister burst into tears when she heard that there were two thousand women and children on board. She had said goodbye to her schooldays and was now a young lady of the world. However, she soon made friends with the ship's officers.

We were sailing in a convoy but not long after we left Liverpool the convoy split up, one half going to Canada and our half bound for South Africa. Alas, our engines developed a problem and accompanied by one submarine we returned to Gourock, Scotland, where the engines were repaired. I remember one of the passengers developing a toothache and only being allowed to go to the dentist with a security officer. No chances were taken.

Our dining-room steward had been torpedoed five times. He made nothing of his adventures and said he soon became used to floating in the water. He was very kind to me because I was a slow eater and would never have had any of the ship's delicious desserts if it had not been for him. He hid my desserts on the porthole shelf and like a conjuror brought them forth when I had finally finished my first course.

We took our boat drills very seriously and had our life jackets with us at all times. Once we were rebuked at breakfast because the ship had had a boat drill in the night and we had slept through the alarm. My mother was frustrated with me because I had friends with whom I played Monopoly day and night. She had to drag me away to see the divers in the West African port of Freetown. I learned that yellow fever was rampant there so I was glad to be safely back on our ship, at anchor in the harbour.

I remember arriving at Cape Town and seeing the harbour and surrounding land dazzling with fairy lights. We had had to observe the blackout in Great Britain and never saw lights twinkling at night. Joyce was delighted when we reached Cape Town because she was reunited with Guy Forte. He was on the troopship HMS *Ormond*, which was in our convoy. The ships had been waiting two weeks for us to arrive so their passengers had had plenty of time to explore the mainland. We only had two days to explore. I remember going to the lovely Mount Nelson Hotel for dinner and seeing Table Mountain with a cloud resting like a tablecloth on its flat top. We took a coach trip round the cape and saw beautiful white lilies growing. I remember the hairpin bends and how the driver took both hands off the steering wheel to show us the size of the fish that were caught in the sea below. I know the driver was enjoying himself but I remember I was scared.

When we left Cape Town it was a tremendous thrill to be again in the company of our original convoy. Six weeks went by very quickly and it was sad to say goodbye to our crew and my favourite steward. That we had made it safely to Bombay was no small miracle. It was a long train journey to Karachi. I remember the sleeper train and waking up in my bunk with sand in my mouth and hair: the Sind Desert had blown into our carriage. The intense heat was a new experience. But nothing mattered except that we would soon be reunited with my father in Karachi.

We never made it to New Zealand. The Japanese were advancing rapidly. Hong Kong, Singapore, and Burma fell and the Japanese reached the borders of Assam, in India. The Allies' ships came limping into Karachi harbour, where they were rehabilitated. The route to New Zealand became a war zone. We had no option but to stay in India.

Three

A Schoolgirl in India

When I arrived in India at the age of twelve my education in Karachi, where we lived, was provided by a series of governesses. This was not because I was such a dreadful child but because the governesses' husbands had been transferred to the war zones. Other families in the non-Indian community were experiencing the same problem and they worked together to organize Miss Hickey's War School.

Miss Hickey was tall and militaristic and waged a one-woman war against the mistreatment of the local donkeys. Donkey and camel carts were the main form of transportation for people and goods in Karachi in the 1940s. While Miss Hickey was content to let the camels look after themselves, she was most concerned at the treatment meted out to the smaller donkeys.

The main thoroughfare used by the donkeys passed by our classroom window. We soon learned that the way to disrupt our class was to inform

Miss Hickey whenever a donkey cart passed by. Miss Hickey would rush out into the street to rescue the poor exhausted underfed thirsty donkey that was pulling a cart containing the driver, his six passengers, and a heavy load of rocks and stones, while being beaten constantly with a stick. Miss Hickey would confront the astonished driver who, as far as he was concerned, was doing nothing he should not do. Her special concern was the bit, which she would remove from the donkey's mouth and bring back to the classroom where it was added to her collection, rather like a gunslinger adding notches to his gun barrel. If we learned nothing else in Miss Hickey's War School, we certainly learned compassion for the hard-working donkey.

Singing was important in our school curriculum. Great energy and enthusiasm went into an annual school concert. For one memorable performance we blacked our faces and sang minstrel songs from the southern United States. I will never forget singing "Old Man River," "Camp Town Race Track," and "Way Down upon the Swannee River." Nor will I forget the singers whose voices carried the show, Colin and Ben Herman,[10] Peter and Hugh Forbes, and June Cullen.

Colin and Ben outgrew Miss Hickey's school and moved on to Sheik Bagh, Tyndall Biscoe Boys' School in Srinagar, Kashmir. I too outgrew Miss Hickey's War School and was sent in 1942 to the Presentation Convent School in Srinagar. The boys' mother, Aunt Petty Herman, took me with them on the momentous journey to our new schools. The trip took us four days and three nights. We went by train from Karachi to Lahore where we spent the night in Filetti's Hotel. We caught a train the following morning to Rawalpindi, staying the night there. The next day we rented a car and driver for the final part of the journey. This took us through spectacular mountain scenery. The driver negotiated horrendous hairpin bends as we looked down on terraced paddy fields and gushing rivers. It was necessary to break our journey, spending a night in a daak bungalow (rest cabin). The next day we reached Srinagar, the end of our journey, and enjoyed a welcome rest at Nedous Hotel. Nedous was owned by a Swiss family whose culinary offerings included delicious cupcakes that I have since seen only in Switzerland. The next day Aunt Petty took the boys to their new school and me to mine.

Not So Jolly Hockey Sticks

At the Presentation Convent School my happier school memories revolve around field hockey. My introduction to the game was precipitated by a loud whistle. A hockey stick was thrust into my hands and I was told to put on my plimsolls, which were with all the other pupils' smelly shoes, in a shoe bin. The two captains selected their teams. As a new girl, an unknown quantity, I was chosen last. I was placed on the field and told where I was to cover the ball and in which direction to hit it. Fortunately, I was a naturally fast runner and soon learned the rules of the game. After this first game I was never again the last to be chosen.

The referee for our hockey games was the only Indian master in the school. He taught Sanskrit and Hindi and was professorial in appearance. One of his students was Karan Singh, son of the maharajah of Kashmir. Unhappily for those of us on the opposing team the referee's whistle was never blown when Karan Singh committed a foul. He could hook our sticks with impunity, allowing one of his team to steal the ball. Another bonus to playing hockey was that we played Tyndall Biscoe School, which meant playing against Colin and Ben Herman. Unlike Karan Singh, the boys of Tyndall Biscoe School played by the official rules even though they thought it was not appropriate to play against girls.

Karan Singh and his colleagues added weight to our team and the Biscoe boys had to use all their tactical skills to escape constant defeat. We had a prince of a goalie in Eileen Flood. When she took up her position, armoured in her shin pads and padded gloves, a Goliath would have trembled. Filling the goal, she dared any opposing ball to enter her territory. On the forward line, Iffat Quayoom, Sheila Uberoi, Elspet MacGregor-Gray, Usha Rhudra, and I speedily carried the ball into Biscoe territory, much to their chagrin. Even when we won, the Biscoe boys admitted that they enjoyed the game. The "hip hip hurrahs" at the end of play were genuine and enthusiastic.

The only opponents who could frustrate Eileen Flood were the nuns. Sister Vincent was the instigator in persuading the other nuns to field a team against us. They had one enormous advantage over us: their habits. Their long black skirts made perfect hiding places for the ball. Sister Patricia, Sister Immaculata, Sister Ignatius, and Sister Vincent – the forward line – looking like penguins, progressed towards the goal. Under one of their habits was the ball. Under which one was only revealed when they shot a goal. Poor Eileen could only guess which nun would kick the ball from beneath her gown and shoot a goal. They were full of tricks and their teamwork was mystifying. A ball kicked out from one nun's gown could be shot into the goal by a second nun in a more strategic position. The referee was no help to us either; he was the visiting priest. I think they had God on their side too.

———

For one term I escaped the convent school dormitory and enjoyed the privacy of sharing a room with Elspet MacGregor-Gray. She was tall with lovely auburn hair and beautiful eyes. She was self-possessed and above all had a great sense of humour. I was the antithesis of Elspet with my short legs, unruly brown hair, and braces. I enjoyed hockey, Elspet did not. I was shy and lacked confidence. Nevertheless Elspet insisted that I had a good figure. I wondered how that would help me in school where learning maths and French were of the utmost importance. Elspet loved to act and had starring roles in all the school plays.[11] I remember her best playing Charlie Chaplin in a school production. I was full of admiration for her acting a man's role, which she did in a great spirit of fun. She had to hide her lovely hair under a bowler hat and wear a tiny moustache, made from boot polish. She had no problem imitating Chaplin's distinctive walk and other mannerisms.

The room we shared was on ground level at the end of the quadrangle, far away from the front entrance and a good distance from the girls' lavatories. The room had a narrow entrance containing two chairs leading into a small bedroom with a bed against the wall on either side of the room. On Elspet's side of the room there was a hand basin and on my side a built-in wardrobe. There was no room for even a bedside table with a reading lamp.

One night I was woken by what sounded like something grinding its teeth in my ear. I always slept with a flashlight under my pillow so that if I had to go to the lavatory in the night I would not disturb Elspet by putting on the main light. To my horror, when I flashed my light on the wall I saw next to my pillow an enormous hairy spider. It was as large as a saucer and took off at great speed from the lighted wall into the darkness.

I had let out a scream on first seeing the hairy spider and this woke Elspet. She saw my flashlight illuminating the wall and wondered what I was doing.

"A tarantula as large as a saucer and hairy!" I gasped. "It woke me because it was grinding its teeth in my ears."

Elspet was alarmed and we were both in shock wondering what to do. We could not turn the light on because the nuns would come down. They would never understand our fear of a spider and we would in all probability be sent back to the dormitory. The privacy of a room was delegated to responsible schoolgirls. Wisely or unwisely, I used my flashlight as a spotlight on the spider, whereupon it took off into the dark on Elspet's side of the room. She had seen it illuminated by my flashlight.

"The broom," she whispered.

There was a broom in the entranceway but who was to get it? Not knowing where the spider might be, we were both too terrified to move. A compromise was reached. I would get the broom and as Elspet was taller, she would use it to flick the spider out into the corridor. The window was closer, but it was barred, and the spider was so wide we doubted whether we could get it between the bars. Then we decided we absolutely could not hurt it as its partner would definitely return to get its revenge. The bristles of the brush, we remembered, were comparatively soft. We could add to the softness by wrapping a black silk scarf that Elspet had borrowed from her mother around the broom head.

So the stage was set. I retrieved the broom, wound the black silk scarf round the brush, and gave it to Elspet who stood poised for action on her bed. I shone the light on the spider, which was now on the ceiling on my side of the room; as we had anticipated, it ran to the dark part of the ceiling on Elspet's side. Now came the first flaw in our plan: Elspet could not see it. We decided we had to put the light on and risk the nuns coming down at three in the morning. Elspet with her first sweep of the brush dislodged the spider. Like a flash of lightning, in two giant steps, with the broom outstretched before her she was through the outer room and had dropped the brush and spider in the corridor. We shut the door and put the blanket we used to keep out the draft back in its place along the bottom of the door. This time we hoped it would keep the spider out as well as the cold air.

We were so nervous after this adventure that we both needed the lavatory. We could not go down the corridor to the lavatory because of the spider so Elsepth, ever resourceful, suggested we use the hand basin. It was fine for her because she had long legs and managed discreetly, but for me it was a major problem. If only I had a chamber pot under my bed. No such luck. I thought of our ram in Karachi and how we had used a brass jug to catch his urine. There was no alternative to the hand basin. I used a chair to get up on the basin and then Elspet turned the chair round so that I could use the back of the chair for support. Alas, for one moment I sat heavily on the basin with my hands holding the sides. The basin gave a creaking sound. I quickly lifted myself up, leaning over the top of the chair, and removed my weight from the basin. At that moment I became aware of my precarious position. What if another spider appeared or the "nun patrol" noticed our light and decided to investigate? What if the basin, abused and weakened, crashed to the floor just as they entered, depositing me onto the cold cement? How would we ever explain ourselves? Elspet remained on guard. She turned off the light. In the dark I lost my spatial perception so Elspet helped me safely down from the hand basin.

We were soon sleeping peacefully in our beds, having arranged that whoever woke first would retrieve the brush and the silk scarf from outside the door. Fortunately, in the morning the nuns went straight to chapel and did not pass by our side of the quad. We hoped that the spider had not become addicted to the silk scarf but had found the large cracks in the corridor walls more to his liking. It became our routine to check for spiders and any other unwelcome visitors before we went to bed so that there would be no more surprise spiders grinding their teeth in the night.

The Show Must Go On

At the approach of our school concert it was required that we all practise singing every day. We sang songs such as "Far from the sea breezes where the seagulls go swimming and diving" and each line had to be repeated again and again. We had to stand and the room would get hot and stuffy. It was all I could do to concentrate on remaining upright. The room's one small window was opened but the door had to remain closed as the volume of our voices would be lost down the corridor. Another item on the concert program was our skittle routine. I now realize that we were brutal to our young instructress from the Teacher Training College in Delhi who had the courage to teach in the nuns' domain.

Twirling skittles was a strange sport. It was supposed to encourage good posture and coordination but we all found it tedious and more entertaining when a skittle came tumbling from a colleague's hand and we were able to laugh. Elspet was the ringleader. She would drop a skittle, which would hit the floor with a resounding crash. Before she had picked up the offending object Heather Coombe would by chance drop one of her skittles and this would cause a chain reaction. The rhythmic class would suddenly be discordant and chaotic. The teacher would turn the gramophone off and amidst muffled laughter we would regroup ourselves, leaving sufficient space between each student to twirl our skittles. We began again in harmony but the situation was soon repeated as another brave person assumed the part of ringleader. Somehow, from this fracas, our young teacher had to train us to put on a spectacular show for the school concert.

The concert this year was being held on the ballroom stage of the exclusive Nedous Hotel on the outskirts of Srinagar. The maharani and maharajah of Kashmir, Karan Singh's parents, had graciously agreed to be present. They were active supporters of the Presentation Convent School and the nuns wanted to put on a topnotch performance for them. Alas, the odds were against the performers. One of my schoolmates developed mumps, and while she was not seriously ill the mumps spread rapidly through the school. We all had painful swollen glands and dewlaps hanging from the sides of our faces. We were allowed to miss classes but we had to get up from our beds and attend singing practice and the infamous skittle rehearsals.

It was impossible to change the date of the concert because it was being held at Nedous Hotel and because the nuns knew that the maharajah and maharani had too many commitments to change their schedule. When the dreaded day came we all sallied forth with alien faces and swollen necks. It was painful singing with swollen glands and we were self-conscious with our ugly dewlaps. To the audience we must have appeared like a new breed of *Homo sapiens* and the parents must have had a difficult time recognizing their offspring. To everyone's relief the skittle performance went. with great precision. No one dropped a skittle and the nuns were delighted. Thankfully the young instructress did not lose her job as she so easily might have. We were relieved that the concert was over and we could stay in bed for the next few days and rest our aching swollen glands.

Hockey to Horses

It was Aileen Van Agnew's idea. In the summer many of us enjoyed two weeks' holiday in Gulmarg, a beautiful hill station in Kashmir where ponies were the only means of travel. We bonded with our ponies and missed them immensely when our holiday came to an end. Back in Srinagar my convent school had a generous stretch of green grass that accommodated two grass hockey fields and could be used, Aileen suggested, to hold a gymkhana with a race track around the outside. Our minds boggled in anticipation. We could erect simple jumps and have a competition. We could even have a simple game of polo. We would invite the maharajah and the maharani and since the maharajah loved horses they would, we felt sure, accept our convent school's invitation to the "horse event." Aileen had the address of the syce whose pony she had hired in Gulmarg. Syces were the owners and caretakers of the ponies. Aileen's syce stayed in Srinagar for the winter and he, we were sure, would be able to contact the other syces. Imagine, we would all have our beloved ponies to ride. In Gulmarg our ponies had attended Mrs Bayer's weekly pony club and Mr Da Souza, who played in the Nedous Hotel dance band, had even played his accordion for us to rehearse a musical ride. My pony, Rani, had been scared by the sounds from Mr Da Souza's accordion. He had kindly come fifteen minutes before the rehearsal to give Rani a solo concert so that she would become used to the unusual sounds and not disrupt the musical ride.

The idea for the gymkhana raised many questions. Would the syces be able to provide us with sufficient ponies? Did Mr Da Souza play at the Srinagar branch of Nedous Hotel in the winter and would he be willing to help us with the musical ride? Would the nuns allow us to hold the special event? How much time would the nuns allow us for practising with our ponies with Mr Da Souza and his accordion?

Aileen continued to spearhead the project and planned a program that she thought would impress the nuns. She had contacted her syce, who was willing to help within his limitations. We planned a musical ride, a short game of polo, a competition that involved riding between poles as in a skiers' slalom race, a jumping competition, and, as a grand finale, a relay race where two teams competed passing a riding crop to the next member of the team.

We asked for an appointment with Mother Peter to discuss the matter. She was a genuinely pleasant motherly nun but admitted that she had no experience with ponies. She pointed out, however, that the ponies' hooves would ruin the hockey field. We countered by explaining that we would not use both playing fields and the relay race would take place only on the edge of both playing fields. She asked us to leave our plan with her and she would discuss it with the other nuns.

Meanwhile, Barbara Reeves, Daphne Mason, and Myfanwy had come up with the idea of a sports day featuring an egg-and-spoon race, a sack race, a three-legged race, a "pin the tail on the donkey" contest played blindfold, and modified pony activities. As an alternative plan Aileen, myself, and the other keen riders were happy to accept their suggestion should Mother Peter reject our own request. When we received a no from Mother Peter we put forward their alternative suggestion for a sports day but asked again for the relay horse race that would not affect the playing fields. Again, Mother Peter needed to discuss our proposition with the other nuns.

While we waited for the nuns to reach a decision interest in the sports day vibrated through the school. Conversation revolved round how to procure chicken eggs to boil for the egg-and-spoon race, how to obtain strong triangular bandages to tie round our ankles for the three-legged race, and where to get large sacks for the sack race. Aileen all the while kept in touch with her syce. We shared memories of the gymkhana in Gulmarg and the weekly pony club. I remembered with sadness seeing Rani in Srinagar pulling a garry with her syce at the reins. I realized he had to make a living in winter to feed her and his family but the sight upset me so much I could not even wave to the syce. I thought of how responsive she was as I learned to jump at the pony club in Gulmarg. Mrs Bayer had complimented me on my improved posture when jumping, but it was only because every time we went over a jump I leaned forward to whisper in Rani's ear "I love you!"

Learning to jump on Rani, my tonga pony, at Mrs Bayer's pony club in Gulmarg. I was told that I had a good seat, but only Rani knew why.

Iffat Quayoom, one of my special friends, in her parents' garden in Srinagar, Kashmir.

As we waited for the nuns' decision we tried to further our cause by appealing to our parents. We realized that Iffat Quayoom, one of the school-girls, was a bonus in this respect because her mother was friendly with the maharani. Twelve years earlier the maharajah had fallen in love with a beautiful peasant girl whom he had seen walking elegantly, balancing a large clay pot of water on her head. He later married her. Before the nuptials Iffat's mother, who was herself very beautiful and charming, had been asked to train the future maharani in the ways of the court down to the simple act of using a handkerchief. They had privately remained good friends. Even if Iffat's mother could not persuade the maharajah and maharani to give us their blessing, Iffat could ask her parents for their support. Many of the other pupils talked to their parents and gradually many became aware of our dream. This proved a danger as well as a blessing.

Pari Rasheed, whose mother lived in Delhi, had a younger sister who went to a convent school in that city. It was run by the same order of Presentation nuns as our school and we feared that Pari's sister might innocently mention our dream of a sports day. Etiquette dictated that Mother Peter should be the first to approach the nuns in Delhi for their approval since the Delhi school had been established before the school in Srinagar.

We were having supper in the dining room when the announcement for which we had been waiting was made. Mother Saviour was walking up and down between our tables, reading her prayer book. We were concentrating so hard on timing her movements, in order to slide undetected the detested semolina pudding into paper bags on our laps, that we did not see Mother Peter enter the room. She rapped on the table for our attention. Mother Peter announced that we could have our sports day and that the details would be discussed with the senior students, the sisters, and Mr Rau, the Sanskrit teacher. We gave her a round of applause, clapping and stamping our feet. Mother Peter sailed from the room smiling, well pleased with herself.

Lady Bird, the older sister of my classmate Bubbles Rawlings, would be one of the seniors included in the planning and we had every confidence in her diplomatic skills. She would be our favoured ambassador. Surprisingly, we learned from Lady Bird that Mr Rau was a great supporter of our sports day as were Mary Brown, the skittles teacher, Father Paul, and the mother superior from the sister convent school in Delhi.

The sisters' immediate task was to seek the approval of the maharajah and maharani who fortunately had already heard of the sports day from their son, Karan Singh. As privileged guests they were to choose the day and time of the event. They chose the first Saturday in September, which fortunately was not a religious holiday for anyone.

The nuns and all the pupils were delighted. Lady Bird and Kamilla, another senior student worked closely with Aileen, who was a little disappointed that we would not have more pony involvement. But she had to be content as the relay race had been accepted as one of the events. Aileen was responsible for contacting the syces and liaising with those of us who wanted to ride our ponies. She suggested there should be twelve riders, six in each team, but the syces paced the area and said that three ponies on each side, making a total of six, would be a realistic number for two competitive teams. Aileen had to agree with them since without their approval there would be no relay race and no pony involvement.

We had a month to do our planning. Rhoda, who was artistic, made a sample invitation. Appropriate spoons were wheedled from Mother Saviour for the egg-and-spoon race. She promised us twelve hard-boiled eggs, which would also be the prizes for the egg-and-spoon race. We needed prizes for all the races and something durable would be needed for the "pass the parcel" prize. The round-the-pole race on ponies had been changed to "musical chairs" and the inclusion of a "bobbing-for-apples" competition was under discussion. Although we were paying the syces Aileen insisted that they and the ponies, winners and losers, should be presented with a rosette by the maharani. The non-riders requested a team for a running relay race, which meant getting prizes for the runners of the winning team. The best and most democratic prize, we decided, was fudge from Lala Sheik. The finances would have to be worked out and the nuns would have to agree, which we knew would be no easy matter.

Mr Da Souza and his accordion would make the musical chairs special. Would he be available and would he be costly? We would need a large tub for the apple bobbing. The prizes would be the apples gripped between the winners' teeth. The obvious prize for "unwrap the parcel" would be a box of chocolates: we were hoping that Mr Da Souza would play his accordion for that too.

Mother Saviour gave us empty dal sacks from the kitchen. We tried them out but Elspet and others with long legs complained that they were not deep enough and were too tightly woven to expand as they needed to for a sack race. There was no substitute for a hessian potato sack. The search was on. We also needed a stopwatch and wise Lady Bird thought we needed someone knowledgeable in first aid in case anyone twisted an ankle or suffered some other injury. Miraculously, Mary Brown, our skittle instructress whom we all loved when she was not getting us to twirl skittles, was willing and fully trained to accept that responsibility. Thus a major hurdle was overcome. We knew there would be last-minute emergencies but we were all prepared for our sports day when Saturday, 2 September arrived. The sun was shining and the event began at 2:00 P.M.

Even the boatmen crossing the Jhelum River had run lines of tiny flags over their mini-shikaras, passenger boats with well-sprung seating for two and a canopy, manned by two paddlers. This made the crossing festive and put their passengers in an enthusiastic mood for our sports day. Jayne Bunbury was the official timekeeper and Sister Vincent her backup for recording the names of the winners. The much-anticipated relay race on the ponies went without a hitch. Fortunately no one fell off even though the ponies developed all the qualities of racehorses and galloped at top speed, not even stopping at the end of the race. Aileen had taken this into account and ensured that there was enough space between the convent and the hockey field for riders to continue galloping without leaving the school grounds or entering the public path onto the bund. Jayne Bunbury had become overwhelmed by the speed of the ponies, but Sister Vincent fulfilled her role as a backup and kept a steady eye on her stopwatch. However, when Jayne Bunbury announced that Aileen's team had come second, Aileen was convinced there had been a human error over the recording of the times. She believed that with her riding Dandy her team had to come in first. Sister Vincent in her pleasant way reassured her that there had been no error and that her team had only lost by five seconds. In fact both teams could be considered winners.

The maharani presented the two teams with rosettes so that no one was aware which was the winning team. We all had a final gallop round the circuit with our ponies wearing their rosettes securely attached to their bridles. Best of all, the syces were beaming with pleasure and our ponies received sugar lumps.

A School Outing

The news at the convent school was that the nuns were hiring a cookhouse that belonged to a houseboat to take us on a school picnic. The plan was to moor the boat in one of the less-frequented lakes near Dahl Lake. I knew the nuns would be careful not to fall in, but what if one missed her footing? No wonder they were hiring a solid cookhouse boat. The picnic was planned for a Saturday so that the Sunday service we attended at the local Roman Catholic church would not be deprived of its organist, Sister Immaculata, or its choir, which was us, some of the boarders. There was a great buzz of excitement in the school as little groups of friends intermingled; the older girls were to be responsible for the younger ones. Rosemary Waring, whose father was a prisoner of war, had a younger sister, Ann, and a young brother, Colin, whom she would be responsible for.

On the Jhelum River en route to Dahl Lake in the cookhouse-type boat that was rented for our school picnic.

Lady Bird would be responsible for her two younger sisters, Bubbles and Bulbul. I was teemed up with Naheed and her sister, Nasheed. They had both wept bitterly during their first days at the convent school, only a month earlier, and with Iffat's help I had tried to comfort them. Now we were going to have fun on an outing. In preparation for the picnic we were told to wear our school uniform (a navy tunic with a white blouse and green girdle), bring a thick cardigan, a change of clothes, a book to read, and precautions against the sun and mosquitoes. We were not to take shorts or bathing costumes. I planned to smuggle four boiled glucose sweets in my pocket to share with Naheed and her sister in the hope of preventing a burst of tears should they feel homesick. At last the day arrived and we were blessed with sunshine. The cookhouse-type boat was moored where we usually boarded the shikara to cross the Jhelum River. The owner of the boat helped us onboard and we watched with delight as the nuns, the last to board, gingerly lifted their habits to step onto the boat.

The anchor, which was a heavy rock secured with rope, was lifted and we were away, drifting with the currents of the Jhelum River. The owner had a large pole which he placed in the water ahead of the boat; then he walked to the back of the boat, hauled it out and, walking forward again, replaced it in the river. His actions were like a modified version of pole vaulting. They also reminded me of paintings of elegant ladies in long dresses and gentlemen in boaters punting on the river in Cambridge. Our cookhouse boat had two men, equally experienced, who shared the punting.

We had never been on this part of the river and it was wonderful to pass so near to the houses along the riverbank. It was picturesque, but the bad smells spoilt the unique scenery. Our polers propelled the cookhouse boat into a lock. The gates closed and we waited for the water to rise. In the lock we were jostled by small shikaras and there was a lot of yelling in Kashmiri, which perhaps fortunately I did not understand. There was also much spitting from the locals in their shikaras. This was accepted behaviour and it was up to us to move should the breeze send the spit in our direction. The beauty of the shikaras loaded with flowers compensated for any unpleasantness. We negotiated three locks, and when the last of the lock gates opened we were level with Dahl Lake, our destination.

On the way there we heard the constant click of the nuns' rosary beads; suddenly the noise stopped. We made for a small island and the nuns told us we had to stay on one part of the island and not roam, since the island was home to a leper colony. After hearing this I was not sure that I even wanted to land, but the other girls thought nothing of it. The mooring safely achieved, we took off our shoes and socks and jumped in the water. We were soon on the grassy banks of the island.

Food was the next memory I have of our unusual picnic. Instead of cucumber sandwiches we were given the most delicious curry, a wonderful change from the usual dal and rice. We had chapatis, freshly baked and warm. The cook had been working while we enjoyed the scenery. There were even second helpings, which made us all very happy. We felt delightfully lazy after lunch and were content to read and write letters home. Later we joined Iffat, Myra Khan, Julia Sherjan, Megan and Joan Scott Russell, Thelma, Margaret Curnew, Jean Urmson, Joan Bragg (another girl whose father was a prisoner of war), and others in a game of catch with tennis balls brought by the nuns. The time went quickly. Naheed and Nasheed enjoyed the open space and happily showed no signs of being homesick. We were a large party and the nuns became anxious as stormclouds gathered. Reluctantly we obeyed their instructions to return to the boat. We were welcomed aboard with a hot cup of milky tea known as chai.

The journey back was equally interesting as we had a different view facing the opposite direction. The wind blew suddenly down from the surrounding mountains, ruffling the water, and we were glad of our extra clothing. Then the rain came teeming down and I felt sorry for the men who had to pole our boat as they had no protection from the weather. The

Mother Peter (left) and Sister Vincent. We believed that the nuns borrowed our bathing suits and swam in the school pool when we were out for our walk.

lock experience was different in the pouring rain and we wondered whether the rainfall would expedite the filling of the lock. Parri Rasheed, always fun to be with, began singing and chanting and we hummed along with her. None of us wanted to return to the convent, but we began to get hungry and we were not going to eat until we were back at the school. Our wonderful cook on the boat had used all the food allocated to her. There were no emergency provisions, and while we had been well fed the fresh air had given us insatiable appetites. Even dal and rice would be welcome.

We could hardly tell where the boat was moored; the shikara taxis that we usually looked for had all gone home. We had confidence in the men who had taken us on our expedition and knew they would not allow us off the boat in the wrong place. The red brick of the school soon came in sight as we climbed up the riverbank in crocodile file. The nuns must have breathed a sigh of relief when their final head count showed that we were all there. It was a special outing, but regrettably it was never repeated during my time at the school. We were limited to Saturday walks along the bund on the same side as the school to avoid the adventure of crossing the river. When we returned from these walks we were hot and wanted to swim in the school pool, but often we found that our bathing costumes were already wet. We were convinced that the nuns borrowed them and frolicked in the swimming pool while we were off on our midday walk. I had a modern elasticized swimming costume and my friends joked that Mother Peter, who was large, must have borrowed mine as it was the only costume that could expand to her size.

Four

At Home in Karachi

Mohammed

In Karachi we had two official government doormen, or puttiwallas. They wore a uniform of red jackets and wide white pantaloons with a red sash around the waist. Mohammed, from Baluchistan, was extremely handsome and a fine red turban added to his height of more than six feet. Ali was short and fat with a grey beard and reminded me of Father Christmas. Mohammedans normally pray five times a day and Mohammed did so in private at the bottom of the garden. I sometimes saw him at his evening and morning prayers when the sunsets and sunrises reflected magically in the surrounding desert. Ali's day was spent in sleep and prayer, which in his case seemed to be identical states. We hesitated to disturb him when he was praying. Thus, when Ali was on duty our visitors received no welcome and were left to their own devices while he collected himself from his

Our home, The Ridge, Bath Island, Karachi. In the foreground people are gathering salt. Behind them is the rugger pitch used by the army.

sleepy meditative state and belatedly rushed ahead of them to the front door. Mohammed, on the other hand, was like a guardsman at Buckingham Palace, attentive to every detail. Car doors were opened, visitors were assisted, and drivers were given instructions for parking. No unannounced visitors arrived on our doorstep while Mohammed was on duty.

As was the custom, Mohammed had left his family in Baluchistan and only saw them on his annual leave. He saved his money for his wife and children. He had a good friend, Raj, another handsome Baluchistani, who looked after the electric generator that supplied the energy for our lights and ceiling fans. They had another chum, the chobidar, an official of the court who walked in front of Pa at the opening of each daily court session carrying the mace. From a distance he looked majestic in his red uniform with its gold braid and his red turban, carrying the mace on a red velvet cushion. Close up he had a wonderfully interesting wrinkled face and only a few teeth, which gave individuality to his smile.

Mohammed was very brave, as we saw on many occasions. One evening we were sitting outside on the verandah before dinner enjoying a long cool drink of lemonade, made from fresh lemons squeezed by our cook and kept cold in the larder. We had no fridge. The early evening was treasured as a light breeze often wafted off the desert that surrounded our house. The dusk was restful to our eyes after the glare of the bright sunlight and the heat that reflected off any window that did not have a blind. During this quiet time we heeded the mysteries of the approaching night, the call of the jackals that lived in the rocky mound on the desert below our house and the stars that came out one by one. In this serene atmosphere I suddenly noticed a distinctive long black shape on the manicured lawn near the verandah where we were sitting.

"A snake!" I gasped.

"Where?" my mother demanded.

We immediately called the dogs, Rex, Bunty, and Sally, before they could pick up the snake's scent and attack it. For once they were obedient, coming immediately, thinking it was their call to dinner. We rewarded them with biscuits and shut them in the study to wait for their meal away from the tempting scent of the snake. Meanwhile Pa called Fernandes, our bearer, who called Lewis. Lewis called our hummel (water carrier), our hummel called the sweepers, but no one wanted to go near the resting snake. Finally Pa called Mohammed, our brave puttiwalla, who without hesitation brought a long stick and hit the snake fiercely on the head. The snake wriggled briefly and then remained motionless. With one blow he had killed it.

He laid his kill on the verandah and we all cautiously approached, hoping it was not just playing dead. Everyone was very relieved by our puttiwalla's success. Then Mohammed pushed the stick under the snake's body and lifted it up again. By now it was dark and we could not see the snake distinctly. But something was wrong. The once apparently solid snake dangled limply and weightlessly over the stick.

Mohammed asked for a flashlight. Not having one ready to hand, Fernandes brought a lighted candle from the dining-room table. Unfortunately the gentle evening breeze blew it out. Fernandes struck a match to relight the candle and even as he was doing this Mohammed recognized his mistake

"No snake, sahib. Rex's lead."

Rex was our cocker spaniel and his great pleasure in the cool of the evening was to rush round the lawn holding his lead in his mouth while we chased him and tried to retrieve it. We often gave up and he would get bored and drop the lead. What a relief. What an anticlimax. Pa had been concerned for the marlies, our gardeners, who enjoyed walking barefoot on the grass while they watered it morning and evening. Now there was no danger for them. We were all laughing and Fernandes, Lewis, our hummel, and our two sweepers, husband and wife, all went away chuckling. Mohammed would have an amusing story to tell his friend Ali when he came on duty in the morning.

Our "Mistry"

In Urdu the word for cook is mistry. Our mistry was handsome, with grey hair and wonderful rich brown smiling eyes. He always had a young assistant from Goa. After being under his tutelage for three years the assistant would leave armed with a great reference and take up a more senior position in another household. Our mistry and his wife were both from Goa and were practising Roman Catholics, a legacy of having been born in a Portuguese colony. He played the violin and accompanied my mother when she played the piano. He and his wife had a pet mongoose that was kept in a cage and let out every so often, especially when I visited them. It took a long time, but eventually the mongoose became accustomed to me and would take a peanut out of my hand. Our mistry and his wife always made me welcome in their home.

I also visited him when he was working in our kitchen. For fun he taught me to rub my tummy and say in Hindustani, "Hamara pate khali hi, pice muncta," which meant, I am hungry and I need money to buy food. I thought this was the greatest fun, pretending to be a beggar.

When my parents gave an elegant dinner party the mistry made the most delicious fudge squares. They were placed on a silver tray in the cooling cupboard, which had a wire mesh front so that one could see through to the candy. The mesh was to keep out the ants but it did not keep me out. I found that if I took one piece of fudge and rearranged the rest no one would notice. The fudge was so "moreish" that I could never stop at one and this meant having to own up to the cook, who would kindly replace them. Sometimes I stretched his patience to the limit and he had to seek the help of my mother in curbing my sweet tooth.

Our cook was an artist in the kitchen. His pièce de résistance was toffee baskets. The toffee was like fine straw, which he wove into baskets complete with handle and then filled with small fruits soaked in cherry brandy and rich cream. My sins forgiven, the cook always saved me one. I would take it up to my room and with a small spoon enjoy every mouthful, with the same thrill as if I were having a midnight feast.

Another of his specialities was cheese straws. He made individual bundles consisting of a circular cheese straw within which were placed several cheese straws reminding me of small editions of the corn we used to rake and stook on the farm in Devon. He also made cheese butterflies. They had cheese pastry bodies, cheese pastry heads with two large eyes made of currants, and delicate wings made of potato crisps. He used to save me one of these – good psychology because then I did not raid his larder. The butterfly was so lifelike that I sometimes had difficulty eating it.

At times I must have been a great nuisance to our mistry. He went to the market every day with his young assistant cook. When my parents gave dinner parties their choice was roast chicken. Our mistry would bring home a live chicken, which was the custom in India. Chickens were not sold dead because it was not known how they had died or how long they had been dead. There was no refrigeration. Although I was never told when a dinner party was on the agenda I had a sixth sense about when there was a live chicken in the kitchen waiting to be killed. I would hear it cackling in its box and see its beady eyes. Before the cook could get his knife to its throat I would run to my mother and beseech her to save the chicken and change the menu. I would take her hand, persuade her to come with me to the cook, and the chicken would be saved. Stuffed tomatoes would quickly be substituted for the roast chicken on the menu. This is how we came to have such an assortment of chickens in our compound.

We had a splendid cock, he strutted proudly around the compound followed by a retinue of hens that I had saved from the cook – White Sussex, Rhode Island Reds, Grey Leghorns. But not one was on a par with his beauty. He had wonderful iridescent green and black silky tail feathers, a red coxcomb, and wattles of rich ruby red. In the morning he would perch on the water pump and, stretching to an unbelievable height, extend his neck and thus his vocal chords and greet the dawn with cock-a-doodle-do. The sweeper was terrified of him: she had once chased a hen off her nest and taken the eggs, but the cockerel would not have any of his harem interfered with and attacked the sweeper whenever she came near him.

Not included in this flock were three chattery guinea fowl. They were grey blue with white polka dots on their feathers. They had tiny heads with blue feathers on their neck, red beaks and coxcombs, and black beady eyes. If they could, they would have held hands; for somehow without even a handhold they moved side by side in a straight line with no glimmer of light between them. They were identical so I do not know if they ever changed places. If one tempted them with grain they came for-

Dear Mistry,

It is very hard to break up our home and say good-bye to faithful servants and friends and it does not make it any easier when one is so far away. I can only say, my greatest comfort when I have been at home with the children has been the knowledge that you - for so many years have been looking after the Sahib's food and cooking for him and studying his wishes.

I thank you for the care and thought you have devoted to your work and the serving which for so many years you have given to our family and even although we are not in India - I shall still feel that you are part of it. belong to our family. Joy Babba & Wendy Babba join me in sending salaams to you and your wife always, your sincere Memsahib Bessie Davi

Our mother wrote this letter to our mistry, thanking him for his thirty years of service. When my mother played the piano, he sometimes accompanied her on his violin. Those were private moments, and neither of them wanted spectators.

ward together in a quickstep. They bent down in unison but would lift their heads at different speeds. They looked fluffy and I longed to hold one in my hands but that was not their style; their feet were constantly pattering under their feather ballroom dresses. They would never break up their threesome chorus line. At night they accompanied the chickens, led by the cockerel, into the safety of their night quarters where no marauding jackal could enter. If the cockerel did sound an alarm in the night one of the servants quickly went to their rescue and chased away the offending intruder.

Thanks to my alertness the cook never had a chance to show his culinary skills with a roast chicken. Because of my caring heart I had the responsibility of looking after the cockerel, his flock of chickens, and the guinea fowl.

Tiny clay guinea fowl with a real polka-dotted guinea fowl feather.

One summer in Gulmarg, Kashmir, my friends Pixie and Heather Bolton had a cabin a short walk from the main entrance to the boarding house where my family was staying. Another friend, Heather Collins, was staying with us and she and I would take our ponies down to visit Pixie and Heather. There used to be a white chicken that also made friends with Pixie and Heather and we used to feed our ponies with apple and give a piece to the chicken. She loved the apple and used to chuckle away in appreciation. Whenever we visited Pixie and Heather, the chicken would come running up to greet us. She seemed lonely and loved our company and also loved the piece of apple we always gave her. We named her Snow White. When Pixie and Heather left Gulmarg, Heather Collins and I continued to visit the chicken. She used to follow us on our ponies to the boarding house, but she never went on the main road.

When it was time to return to Karachi we did not want to leave Snow White behind as we knew she would be dinner for the snow leopards, so we first asked my mother if we could take her home with us. She agreed but did not want any unnecessary expense. Miss O'Connor, who owned the boarding house, readily agreed to let us take the chicken. We found an old tiffin basket for Snow White to travel in. This we left beside Pixie and Heather's cabin, so that Snow White would become familiar with her new home. When we went to give her the daily apple there was our chicken Snow White sitting happily in the basket.

By the time we were to leave Snow White was happy to have the lid closed on her and she was transported safely to Srinagar. There we hired a car to take us on the dramatic journey to Rawalpindi. In the car we lifted up the lid of the basket to enable Snow White to get some fresh air. Alas, she was horribly carsick and her head was contorted in every direction. We felt miserable for her. Our overnight stop at the daak bungalow gave her time to recover and she survived the rest of the car journey. When we transferred to the train, we let her out of the basket in our private toilet. She promptly sat on the basin and cackled to her reflection in the mirror.

The ticket inspector suddenly arrived and we were nervous that he might want to investigate the strange noise coming from our toilet. My mother had said she was willing to buy tickets for our dogs, Bunty and Rex, but definitely not for the chicken. We knew the ticket inspector would be glad of a chicken dinner, but miraculously the chicken was suddenly silent.

Safely home in Karachi Snow White happily joined our motley collection of chickens. She became a welcome provider of eggs and then to our amazement she became broody. In due time she hatched a family of delightful baby chicks. The cockerel made sure we realized he was the proud father and he went strutting round her guarding every chick. Mrs Clapham, a knowledgeable poultry keeper, was invited up to visit Snow White and her entertaining family. She definitely had no pedigree according to Mrs Clapham but our Kashmiri Snow White was a welcome addition to our menagerie.

For the Love of Birds

Pa had a large collection of birds, and caring for them involved a strict morning ritual. Every morning each birdcage was taken out of Pa's birdroom and placed on the lawn, which was surrounded by a hedge. This called for teamwork since it was important not to leave the birds alone outside. Even in their cages they could be attacked by hawks or beset by other dangers of which we were not even aware. The team, Pa and I, Mohammed, and his friend Raj who looked after the electrical generator, would take ten minutes to perform this mission. One person took a birdcage out and then waited for the next team member to arrive before returning to fetch another cage. We took the trays out of the bottom of the birdcages and the grass would pop through the wires. This grass was the birds' delight. They pecked at the tender shoots and bathed their faces in the early morning dew. Pa watered them with the fine spray from his watering can.

My Indian green parrot with a bright ring of red feathers round his neck stood poised with his wings outspread, waiting for Pa to spray him. When Pa moved on to give the other birds a shower the parrot would screech so loudly that in order to appease him Pa rapidly gave him a second shower. The green barbet enjoyed his early-morning shower but he kept on the move as if he was flying through the jungle, where the spray would fall off the leaves of the tree, giving the barbet a continual gentle shower.

The mynah birds with their glossy black feathers and their bright orange bills and legs would say "Good morning" immediately the spray ceased. It was their way of asking for more. Then there were the tiny birds, Bengalese or Society finches as they are sometimes called. They would sing and sing, whether they were being showered or not. The Java sparrows, so elegant with their grey feathers brightened by red round their black lively eyes, flew in and out of the spray. All Pa's birds had ten minutes to sun and dry themselves and then the trays were replaced and cages carried back to the birdhouse.

Pa himself gave his birds their food and water. He blew off the empty seed shucks and refilled the seed containers. The green barbet had a delectable diet of dates, banana, and pawpaw. My parrot was given special treats, grapes and hot green chillies. He never left a grape for later but I often gave him another one at lunchtime. Pa gave them fresh water in separate containers, one for bathing and another for drinking. Birds can live longer without food than without water, so water is very important. When all the birds had been cared for I went with Prague, our driver, and Pa to court. On returning I would care for the other animals. My mother never resented the amount of time Pa gave to his birds: "As long as they are the feathered kind," she was often heard to say.

One morning Pa and I went into the birdhouse to find one of his Java sparrows flying about its cage calling hysterically. Where was its mate? We went speedily to investigate and there on the floor of the cage was the problem, a snake slithering and gulping with a swollen throat. Alas, the

Java sparrow's companion was now inside the snake, creating a bulge that made the snake too broad to slip through the bars by which it had entered. There was no time to be lost. I rushed to get Mohammed while Pa took the cage into a small adjacent room. While he was wondering what to do Mohammed entered carrying a large stick. Bravely and with great confidence he put his hand in the cage and grabbed the snake behind the swelling in its throat. Out popped the Java sparrow, unharmed but pulsating with fright. Pa quickly picked up the bird before the snake lunged at it again. He kept it warm in his hand while Mohammed dropped the perplexed snake to the ground and hit it on its head with his strong stick.

I thought it was still alive but our puttiwalla explained that it was the reflexes of its body that made it move about; after a few minutes of slithering it remained quiet, truly dead. Mohammed, however, was not satisfied. He thought that if the snake's mate was somewhere around, it would come looking for it and perhaps make a tasty meal of one of the already scared Java sparrows. A mongoose is the best deterrent to a snake but they too would eat our birds, so in this case a mongooose was not a solution. When the birds had all been taken out for their morning bath, Pa and the puttiwalla made a detailed inspection of the birdhouse to see where the snake might have entered. They found no obvious point of entry so Pa suggested that the birdhouse roof and floor be lined with a material similar to linoleum. There was always the fear that a snake could slither in through the door when it was open but there was a limit to the precautions one could take. Pa put the Java sparrows in a cage with wires that were closer together in the hope that no snake could get in.

The sparrows survived their traumatic experience. I believe they found solace in each other's company. They looked so handsome with their grey feathers touched with red below their eyes, orange bills, and red legs and feet, the female dusky compared to the bright red of the male. I am still haunted by the horrors they were subjected to by the slithering large-mouthed snake.

———

At the bottom of our garden in Karachi Pa bred white ants to feed his baby partridges. Breeding white ants was a lengthy procedure. Pa chose the bottom of the garden because it was rocky and dry and, in keeping with my mother's wishes, as far away from the house as possible. My mother was convinced the white ants had a secret path from Pa's breeding area to the house, where they attacked the treasured furniture she and Pa had received as wedding presents and brought with them from England. Pa was convinced that this was impossible and continued to breed the ants for the baby partridges as this was their required food.

Selecting three planks of wood and laying them on the dry ground, Pa watered them morning and evening with the fine spray from his watering can. After three weeks came the magic moment to turn the wood over. There in the moist underpart of the wood were glistening white gelatinous eggs, reminding me of minute frog spawn. For Pa these eggs were more precious than diamonds. The timing was perfect because two of the baby partridges had hatched and there were three more on the way. The male and female partridges were good parents and kept their eggs warm, taking it in turns to sit. If all went as planned there would be five baby partridges in three days' time.

With a knife Pa scraped a portion of the white glistening ant eggs off the wood into a jam jar, and we went with our gift to the partridge family. Pa lifted up the end of the wire netting run and transferred the ants' eggs into the food containers. The male partridge came to the feeder. He expressed his delight by making throaty sounds and raising his neck and head feathers at finding not the usual seed but succulent ant eggs. Having partially digested the eggs he regurgitated them, making them more tasty for the chicks and the mother. The female partridge remained on her nest keeping her two baby chicks and the three unhatched eggs warm. Pa then gave the partridges some fresh lucerne and we went away delighted that we had given the partridges a delicious meal. Two more planks of wood were made ready as Pa had to be prepared for the developing appetites of the baby partridges.

These black partridges were the very ones Pa had given my mother as a birthday present in retaliation for the time my mother had given him a pair of pearl earrings for his birthday. When this occurred my mother said that he had the best of the bargain since her pearl earrings did not call out early in the morning, waking her, the servants, and their families. Now the partridges were causing more matrimonial problems because Pa was breeding white ants and my mother was trying to stop the ants from eating the furniture in the house.

Keeping pheasants as pets was another hobby that Pa was introduced to in India. Breeding is part of the pheasants' natural cycle and when kept as pets it is essential that their diet be as natural as possible. The pheasant's natural diet is high in protein, which pheasants in the wild would obtain from a diet of grasshoppers. While Pa's pheasants would have been prepared to forage in the surrounding forest, Pa was unwilling to risk the dangers of the jungle. Mablaishwar was a small town not far from where we lived in Karachi that boasted a golf course. The greens, fairways, and tees were lovingly watered morning and evening by the marlies with their watering cans. The result was grass that was green and luscious, the perfect home for grasshoppers. The members of the club with their critical eyes oversaw the operation from the clubhouse as they drank their "chotapegs," constantly calling "Quoi hi" for refills.

Pa, who did not play golf, walked around the golf course listening to birdsong, disturbing the grasshoppers. Ever resourceful, he recognized the potential for food for his breeding pheasants. Armed not with golf clubs but with a jam jar, he set off on his hunt. From the clubhouse, the golfers were treated to the sight of a dignified gentleman crouching and leaping at the edge of the fairways. The club secretary, who had given Pa permission to gather grasshoppers, informed the members that this was the local judge gathering food for his pheasants. The sight of Pa leaping about raised their ire: the sacrosanct course was for playing golf, not for catching grasshoppers. Why did he not play golf? they wanted to know.

Since Pa considered golf to be a silly game, they had to satisfy themselves by mocking his activities. Keeping any bird as a pet in India called for devotion and ingenuity, two qualities Pa had in abundance, and he considered a little ridicule a small price to pay for the good health of his birds.

Pa Serenades a Snake

There was no running water in our household so in order to have a bath our hummel brought buckets of hot water to the bathroom and emptied them into the tub. Pa was the only member of the family privileged to take a bath every day. When he returned tired, hot, and sweaty from his day in court, our hummel would prepare the bathwater. He also left a large brass jug of cold water in case the water was too hot.

Having a bath was a serious ritual and there was no lingering about. Once the hot water was in the bath Pa leapt in quickly before it could cool. On this particular day, our hummel had inadvertently spilled some of the water on the floor and Pa had added to it by splashing, dropping his sponge, facecloth, and soap overboard. By now the floor was treacherously wet. Pa always enjoyed his bath and would sing loudly such songs as "Drink to Me Only with Thine Eyes and I Will Pledge with Mine."

This evening while Pa was serenading himself in the bath, he noticed movement where he had dropped his clothes. From beneath this pile a snake slithered across the wet bathroom floor. It took its time, enjoying the feel of the water on its parched body. Then to Pa's annoyance, it slithered back into the pile of clothes. What to do? If he called my mother to come with a fresh set of clothes, he would have to explain why he needed them, and she might faint from shock. This could frighten the snake into biting her. It might even slither into the bath with him! So he went on singing softly to calm himself and perhaps hypnotize the snake as a snake charmer does with his flute playing.

As the bath water began to get cold Pa grew restless.

My mother called, "Godfrey, hurry up in the bath! We promised to have an early supper with Wendy ... Why are you taking so long?"

He dared not call back for fear the change in his tone of voice would frighten the snake. But if he did not reply, my mother might come to investigate. Unfortunately, his pile of clothes was between the bath and the dressing-room door. But fortunately, the door to the back stair, his only escape route, was at the end of the bath. His towel, alas, was hanging on a hook above his clothes: if he grabbed it, he might alarm the snake.

There was no alternative. Pa would have to go starkers down the back stairs. He was still anxious that my mother would return to find out why he was taking so long. Speed was important. Singing all the while "Drink to Me Only," Pa slithered to the end of the bath, stretched to reach the handle of the back door, then leapt from the bath onto the hot metal of the back stair. He grabbed the rail and rushed down, hoping not to meet the snake's mate. Now in full view of the servants' compound Pa saw our sweeper's husband peacefully smoking his hookah. Then the sweeper saw this naked body streaking through his domain. He called his wife but by the time she had come, Pa was out of sight. At the front door Mohammed, our puttiwalla, had knelt to say his prayers. Pa was through the door before the perplexed servant could rise from his knees. It was dusk and Mohammed was not sure whether the naked apparition was a dream or a nightmare. He recovered, however, and gave chase, rushing after the naked intruder. By this time Pa was giving my mother the shock of her life, flying starkers into their bedroom. "Godfrey, what has happened to you?" "A snake in the bathroom," he gasped.

My mother understood. She found him a towel in the linen cupboard outside the bathroom and soon life was back to normal. Not so for the servants. My mother had to calm our hummel, our sweeper, our putti-walla, the head butler, and even our cook. Truly, she assured them, their employer had NOT become a streaking high court judge.

Pa, now fully dressed, gave instructions that the outside bathroom door be left open and that no one was to go into the room until morning. He was hoping that by then the snake would have found a more appropri-ate residence. Our sweeper was also told that if she forgot, entered Pa's bathroom to empty the toilet, and was bitten by the snake, it would be her misfortune as she had been warned. Fortunately my mother's toilet room had a "thunder box" and a hand basin, which my parents would now share. This necessitated more attention from the sweeper.

That was not the end of the story. The next day there was an argument as to whether it was the sweeper's job or the hummel's to see if the snake had vacated Pa's bathroom. Pa had already left for court so my mother had to deal with this. My mother said she would go with a stick and see if the snake was under the bath. Our puttiwalla, butler, and second butler decided they would accompany the memsahib. It was Mohammed who bravely went first and handled the exploratory work with the stick. The snake had gone, with any luck down the back stair. However, our putti-walla had found a hole where the snake could have gained entrance and so he blocked it up. My mother was extremely grateful to him.

Pa knew how stories got magnified and he seemed relieved that noth-ing had appeared in the local paper. Or, knowing Pa, perhaps he was dis-appointed – no heading in the local newspaper, "Chief Judge Escapes Cobra's Fangs by Running Naked from His Bathroom to the Safety of the Servants' Compound."

Two Chinkaras, Dogs, a Deer, and a Lamb

When people came to visit us they never knew what animal might greet or charge them in the grounds or at the door. It might be the dogs, Rex, Bunty, or Sally, Beauty the spotted deer or Larry the lamb; Flopsy and Cottontail, the rabbits; the three guinea fowl or our spirited cockerel who attacked visitors on occasion; or Harry and Harriet the chinkaras, or Indian gazelles.

Bunty was a mongrel given to me one day in Karachi when I was out for a walk by a couple who were desperately trying to find homes for their dog's litter. Once home, and after many tears, I was allowed to keep her. Pa had said we were to have no dogs in India because of the fear of rabies and now we had three.

One winter in Srinagar, Kashmir, when my mother had rented a houseboat on the Jhelum River so that I could go as a day girl to the convent school, a famous botanist, Mr Ludlow, was living on the neighbouring houseboat. He spent his summers in Tibet with another botanist, Mr Sherriff, and they found rare specimens and sent them back to the Natural History Museum in London.[12] Mr Ludlow was not married and he found the plains of India too crowded. Srinagar, which was a summer holiday resort, was devoid of tourists during the winter, which suited his reclusive nature. My parents said the only reason Mr Sherriff was married was that he had found a woman who was willing to hang on to the end of his rope as he attempted to obtain rare alpine plants growing on precipitous mountain ledges in Tibet.

Mr Ludlow loved Bunty. He helped me rescue her when she became too excited and chased three cackling chickens into the Jhelum River. We hung on to a branch and I balanced on one foot while Mr Ludlow held my belt so that I could get my fingers into Bunty's collar and bring her safely ashore. Not having webbed feet, the chickens were swept helplessly downriver. The cook had to go a considerable distance before he retrieved the

My mother with Vicky in Srinagar. It was said that my mother had the best ankles in India, even better than Lady Mountbatten's.

terrified, squawking fowl. It took some time for their egg laying to resume. Mr Ludlow insisted that Bunty was a Lhasa terrier and he persuaded my mother, who persuaded Pa, to have her married to another Lhasa terrier.

By advertising we finally found a suitable husband for her in Rawalpindi. The appropriate time came for Bunty to have her puppies but she did not seem to be gaining weight. Pa took her to the vet who claimed that she would not have any puppies. He was proved wrong. That very night Bunty, who was sleeping on the foot of Pa's bed, gave birth to one beautiful pup, Vicky. We were staying at Miss O'Connor's Boarding House in Gulmarg where the other guests were as interested as we were in Bunty's forthcoming progeny. At last, in answer to their daily questions, Pa was delighted to announce to the other guests at breakfast in the dining room that the long-awaited birth had taken place. The news was greeted with great joviality and Pa was asked if his midwifery skills could be called upon on should any of their pets find themselves *enceinte*.

When Lord Wavell was viceroy of India, he and Lady Wavell came on a visit to Karachi. Pa greatly respected the Wavells, but I am afraid that Vicky and I inadvertently caused them more than a few problems. During their visit Lord Wavell's aide-de-camp fell in love with Vicky and we allowed him to take her on his return with the Wavells to Viceregal Lodge in Delhi. The Wavells also loved Vicky but her behaviour left much to be desired. She would make puddles under the throne on which Lady Wavell was sitting so it looked as if Lady Wavell was the culprit. The poor ADC had to mop up the puddles as quickly as possible. One day no telephone calls came in or out of Viceregal Lodge. It was finally discovered that Vicky, with her sharp puppy teeth, had bitten through the telephone wires. The ADC's job was never dull with Vicky around, and despite her mischievous behaviour the Wavells and the ADC continued to love her. We thought we had found the perfect home for her, wintering in Delhi and going to the Simla Hills in the hot summer. Sadly, Vicky caught distemper and died much too soon.

Harry and Harriet, our two delightful chinkaras, had I think been given to Pa by a zemindar. The zemindars, landowners, were always having "shoots" and offering my family venison, which they considered a delicacy. Pa would receive no such gifts and perhaps a zemindar avoided the gift of dead animals by giving Pa a pair of live gazelles. They were beautiful animals with sand-coloured coats, fine features, eyes with long lashes, and sharp horns protruding from small, bony heads. Their large velvety ears were constantly on the move and when alarmed their delicate tails went up, displaying a white patch on their rumps. Their legs were so fine that their black hooves looked like clumsy black boots.

At night they were kept in a small stable and when we let them out in the morning they leapt into the air, once, twice, three times and more, springing as though on a trampoline high into the sky and landing on four feet to spring again. Rex, our cocker spaniel, would get excited and follow them but he could not keep up and soon gave up the chase. I used to take them a sheaf of lucerne, an Indian clover, and they would come running to have their early-morning "choti hajari," their small breakfast.

I do not know whether Harry was scared of my mother or attracted to her good legs and ankles, but he used to enjoy giving her a surprise butt from the rear when she was not expecting it. Immediately she turned round, instead of charging her again as he would another male chinkara, he would retreat and leap into the air, the beginning of a series of jumps, and pretend innocence. It was a game he played and fortunately my mother was never hurt. Harriet was milder and gentler by nature. I always had to make sure she received her share of lucerne; for Harry would nudge her away with his sharp horns and she would be too scared to return.

They both loved leaping over small hedges and fences. The marlies doing their early watering ignored them but to an onlooker the morning activities in our garden were like a ballet, the two chinkaras leaping together in unison with the two marlies watering. The chinkaras leapt round the marlies but they did not get wet because the marlies never raised their watering cans above waist level. Harriet and Harry caused the marlies distress by pulling down tree boughs and robbing them of their leaves. We gave them more lucerne but the leaves on the tree had a special succulent flavour that the lucerne lacked. The tree survived its ordeal but the chinkaras had to wait a long time for fresh new leaves to replace the ones they had eaten. The chinkaras' leaping ceased when the heat of the sun drove them to find a cactus bush on stony sandy soil out of the sizzling rays of the sun. Here they rested and digested their morning meal. Like cattle they regurgitated their food and chewed happily while flicking the annoying flies that gathered round their eyes. In the evening when the sun set they went into their stable. I believe they realized it was for their safety as they always went peacefully. We rewarded them with two bowls of water and two bowls of grain and dates for a special treat. They also had a block of pink rock salt that they licked to obtain their much-needed supply of salt.

In the wild the growth of their hooves would be kept down by constant leaping on rocky terrain. We made sure they frequented the bottom of the garden where there was a natural wilderness of sand and rocks. Their horns posed no problem because they did not curl inwards but went straight up in a wonderful spiral design.

Harry did not like strangers and always came on them unexpectedly. Although he did not hurt them he gave them a fright by pretending to charge and sometimes touching their legs with his horns. When he was on duty at our house, the puttiwalla, normally so sedate, often had to restrain Harry or one of the other animals from charging a guest. In his efforts to do so his red uniform took on a life of its own, making him look like a large red ball from which his turban flew like a meteorite.

Beauty the deer came into our lives after Pa had taken me to visit the Karachi Zoo. There I saw a herd of beautiful spotted deer like the ones in "Snow White." I said how wonderful it would be if we had a deer to run with the chinkaras. "They would not be friends," was Pa's response. Pulling some leaves, I fed the deer who gathered around me, all the while chatting about how we could give a good home to a deer and how happy it would be. One of the zoo officials must have heard me because he said to Pa, "Let the Missy baba have a deer. They make delightful pets."

Pa was not convinced, but later the zoo official took us to our car and managed to persuade him to accept a deer. When we arrived home Pa told me to get a stall ready. He then had to break the news to my mother who did not want another pet to strike fear into our guests.

Beauty duly arrived and she was so nervous I was afraid she would slip in the stall and break one of her delicate legs. I sat with her for hours, leaving her food on the floor because she would not take it from my hand. Gradually she became used to my smell and less afraid.

Larry the lamb had been brought to us from the market one day by Mohammed and the chobidar who accompanied Pa to court. I had raised Larry in the house, but when he became more self-assured we took him into the garden. There he met Beauty, who immediately became fond him. It was like Shakespeare's *Midsummer-Night's Dream* with Beauty as Titania and Larry as Bottom. They were devoted to each other, inseparable, and everywhere that Beauty went Larry was sure to follow. They were an incongruous couple; Larry grew into a large woolly fat-tailed Dumba ram with curly horns while Beauty was a sylphlike deer. Like Bottom Larry was always gentle with Beauty. Once Larry was weaned he shared accommodation with her in a stable in the compound.

While other people walked their dogs I took Beauty and Larry to visit the gun emplacements manned by three or four British soldiers who were positioned a quarter of a mile from our house. We made a pleasant diversion for the soldiers and although Beauty was hesitant to make friends with them, Larry loved having his head scratched, especially behind his horns. Sometimes his way of thanking was to give a friendly butt on departure. The soldiers learned to wrestle with Larry and so saved their shinbones from being battered. The homeward journey was rapid because Beauty and Larry knew they would be rewarded by fresh luscious lucerne when we arrived.

Lewis and the Matchmaker

When Ayah's foster son Lewis grew into manhood in our household it was decided that he needed to find a suitable wife. Since Lewis was one of the few Goanese Christians in Karachi, he was packed off for a holiday to Bombay, which was closer to Goa. There he was to make an appointment with a matchmaker who, it was hoped, would find him a suitable wife. The whole household was excited and preparations were made to welcome Lewis and his young bride home to Karachi. The cook made a beautiful wedding cake for the occasion. But it was not to be. Lewis returned without a wife.

"What happened?" my father asked. "Did the marriage broker not introduce you to anyone?" "Oh yes," Lewis replied. "I stayed ten days in Bombay and met ten different young ladies but none suited me." My father understood. The timing was not appropriate. "Would you like to go next year?" he asked. "Oh yes," Lewis replied.

So it was that my parents bought a train ticket and two returns from Bombay the next year. They also paid for Lewis's accommodation in Bombay and the marriage broker's fees. Again a fever of excitement went through the household and our cook made another wedding cake.

Lewis set off from Karachi by train and reached Bombay three days later. We received a letter saying he had arrived safely and was enjoying the change. We presumed the change was made more enjoyable by his meeting lovely Goanese girls, one of whom would be his future lifelong companion.

The day came for Lewis's return. Everyone was ready to greet Lewis and his new wife. Alas, again Lewis returned without a wife. "No luck?" my father asked. "They were too fat, too thin, no sense of fun." No one appealed to Lewis. My father realized that the chemistry was not right. Perhaps Lewis needed more time. "Next year?" my father asked, thinking third time lucky.

"Yes, yes," Lewis replied, glad to escape from the disappointment he had caused our extended family. The cook was not having the wedding cake he had specially made eaten without a special occasion. He spoke with my father concerning the prospect of Lewis's meeting a congenial lady; he thought this could happen more informally at the Catholic church that the head bearer, the cook, their wives, and Lewis himself attended. The cook thought Lewis would have more confidence with the support of his friends. They of course would be tactful; for if Lewis learned of this idea he would immediately refuse to go to church. The icing on the wedding cake was changed and the more subdued new icing made the cake unrecognizable. The cook decided they would have a birthday celebration for Lewis after the church service and the congregation would be welcomed with coffee and cake.

Lewis's annual pilgrimage to Bombay was becoming expensive for my parents, apart from the disappointment it caused everyone. A year passed and Lewis had not met a suitable young lady in his church. Once again he set off to Bombay with my parents' blessing. Ayah, now retired and living in Goa, was not pleased with Lewis's obstinacy in his search for a wife. She wrote to encourage him to make a choice. Fortunately the other servants all seemed to be happily married and it was only Lewis who put a strain on my parents' finances.

I believe Lewis went a total of six times to Bombay and then decided he did not want to go any more. He was not lonely because he had the companionship of the other Goanese servants.

He even went on a holiday to Goa with the cook and his wife. There he met up with Ayah. Although he met many lovely people on his holiday he still did not find his dream lady. By the time my sister and I came to India in 1940, Lewis was still happily single.

After partition in 1947 my father felt that he could no longer serve India and our family returned to England. Lewis and all our extended family of servants, after thirty years with my parents, sadly had to find other employers. We received letters from them and kept in touch. Lewis did not manage well on his own without his friends the cook, the bearer, and their respective wives. He must have been lonely. A loving wife, fat or thin, beautiful or ugly, might have helped him in the transition away from his friends. He had obtained a good job with a respected Parsee family in Bombay. They treated him well. He had no complaints until he became very ill with malaria and the family showed little compassion.

He wrote asking for money and again my parents complied. How we wished we were nearer and that he had a good caring Goanese wife to share his later years.

Of Scorpions and Locusts

In Canada in the fall I take pleasure in raking the golden scented damp fallen leaves. Then with my hands I gather them into a wheelbarrow to spread as mulch on the flower beds keeping the plants warm during the winter months. This is a pleasant, peaceful occupation, especially since there are no hazardous insects hidden in the leaves. It was different at our home in Karachi, where I was taught always to shake my shoes and turn them upside down before putting them on in case there was a sleeping scorpion inside. I wore sandals that had a pattern cut into the leather uppers, but you couldn't quite see through the holes to any scorpion that might be nestled inside. I became forgetful sometimes and put my hand in to check for unwanted insects in my shoes. Once I did this and there was something. I screamed from fright but not because I had been bitten. How embarrassed I was when Anne, always at the ready, discovered it was only a large harmless cockroach that she captured and put on the outside stair.

Although my mother ran a peaceful household and attended to everyone's needs, the sweeper family always made discord. The lady sweeper was hard-working but her husband was lazy, and though he was paid to share the duties, he spent most of his time smoking his hookah. His wife not only did his share of the work but cooked, cared for their children, cleaned their home, and was the mainstay of their family. They already had three young children and there always seemed to be another on the way. Sometimes there were loud argumentative voices in the compound, but usually the boy Fernandes, who was known for his conciliatory powers, dealt with the matter. This time the sweeper lady was screaming and my mother realized it was not from temper; not knowing what the problem was she called Fernandes. He already knew the problem, as did the rest of the servants. The lady sweeper had been bitten by a scorpion and was in great pain.

My mother immediately called our doctor, Colonel Emerson, and asked if he would come immediately or recommend treatment over the telephone. He suggested that my mother give the sweeper a painkiller and take her to the hospital as soon as possible: a scorpion's bite could be fatal.

My mother arranged for Prague, our driver, to take her to the hospital immediately, but who was to accompany her? Her husband could not go because he had to stay with their three young children. Then there were all kinds of caste problems. Christians maintained that being baptised as Christians made everyone equal in the eyes of the Lord and believed that this would do away with the caste system. Gandhi did not accept the caste system, insisting that his wife do the lowest of jobs like emptying the commodes, which was the designated work of the sweeper class; neither Christian ideology nor Gandhi's principles had been accepted by our servants or by the rest of the Indian population. My mother did not want to embarrass Fernandes by asking him to accompany our sweeper to the hospital; she knew he would refuse and then ask Lewis, the junior bearer, and Lewis would ask the hummel, and so it would go down the line of caste seniority. Fortunately Anne understood the situation and offered to take the lady sweeper to the hospital. Meanwhile, my mother made cold compresses from an old sheet and wrapped them round the sweeper's dreadfully swollen left hand and arm. Aspirin was the strongest painkiller she had and the sweeper willingly swallowed two between her continuing screams of pain. Because of the pain the sweeper did not need much persuasion to go with Anne and Prague to the hospital. My mother telephoned the hospital and spoke with the nurse of the doctor Colonel Emerson had recommended.

Indian hospitals were always confusing, there were so many people milling about. My mother had tried to streamline Anne and the sweeper's arrival so that they would get immediate attention. My mother was confident that Prague would be assertive and Anne would not allow any time to be wasted. At the hospital the recommended doctor gave our sweeper an injection and told her to rest her swollen left arm and keep it elevated. She was given pills to take every hour. It would be at least three days before she could do any work.

My mother was grateful to Anne and Prague for taking care of the sweeper at the hospital but once home it was her husband that was the problem. Pa said this was an opportunity for him to do his share of the work. My mother knew how surly and unpleasant the sweeper's husband would be and that he would disrupt all the other servants. In my mother's usual tactful way she sought a compromise, asking that the commodes be emptied only once a day. On this occasion we would pour Lysol into the commodes to destroy the germs. We had no running water, hence no flushing toilets, and the sweeper's job was of the utmost importance. Although we were not sure how much rest the lady sweeper had, the pain and swelling did subside, as the doctor predicted, after three days and all was comparatively peaceful in our household once again.

This saga increased my fear of scorpions and made me more careful to check my shoes. Scorpions are the colour of sand and enjoy the warmth of the midday sun on the dusty ground. When the sweeper was using her long straw broom she unknowingly swept up the sleeping scorpion. Instead of using a dustpan and brush she gathered the dust and sand in her hands to transfer into her rubbish bucket, waking the now-frightened scorpion which reacted by stinging her. Her young children were in constant danger from scorpions, for how could she possibly stop them running their hands in the dust and sand on the ground? Yet miraculously they grew up without having their mother's horrendous experience.

———

Black clouds, in Canada, can be a warning of different hazards – snow, rain, thunderstorms, even tornadoes. In India they mean only one thing: locusts, swarms of locusts. At the age of eleven I had never seen or even read about a locust. Grasshoppers, yes, but they were delightful insects jumping off one's hand and then making intriguing noises that one thought would make it easier to find them in the grass. But of course they were teasing, knowing they were beautifully camouflaged and hidden from the human eye. Locusts, I learned, were of the same species. I could not understand why the marlies, our two gardeners, were going berserk, demanding sheets from my mother to cover the plants and the precious grass. My mother was not used to being bombarded by the usually dreamy flower-loving marlies.

"More sheets, memsahib," they demanded. "Quick, quick, quick! Locusts, locusts, locusts! KILL KILL KILL." It was like preparing for a war.

I rushed outside with the marlies and soon we were covering everything in the garden with the sheets. The other servants, ignoring the barriers of the caste system, came and helped, united in their efforts to protect our garden from the invaders. To me it appeared a great mystery and inwardly I found the preparations humorous. To a North American it would seem that we were preparing for ghostly Halloween. I thought the garden looked like the domicile of a dhobi (laundryman) who had put the clean laundry on the ground to dry. There had never been such activity and bustle. Suddenly the innocent sundial was receiving the marlies' wrath because it took up too much sheet and the marlies could not lay the cloth flat. They solved the problem by placing the precious sheets round the sundial and covering their brightly coloured tobacco plants. We found rocks from the bottom of the garden and used them like tent pegs, hoping the locusts would not be able to get under the sheet to feed on the much-treasured grass.

The animals had all been housed as I feared the locusts might change from herbivores into carnivores if they could not have their delicious vegetarian diet. We had run out of sheets and were reduced to pillowcases and even mosquito nets.

My mother had complied with the marlies' wishes and had thrown caution, and the thought of the dhobi's bill, to the wind. We were all so engrossed in our task of covering the garden with the sheets that we had not realized darkness was upon us; the locusts descended like a shower of tennis balls, only larger. They were as large as one's hands. I rushed for my tennis racquet and pretending I was practising my serve tried to locate a locust and crash down on it. But unlike a tennis ball they were unpredictable and moved in every direction. I changed from the normal style of dignified tennis and threw my racquet up in the air as I had seen the players do at Wimbledon at the end of a match. No luck. The racquet descended without capturing or killing a single locust. I learned later that I was lucky the locusts had not devoured my racquet, with its wooden frame. The garden was black, the whiteness of the sheets disappearing beneath thousands of locusts. They ignored our efforts and ate through the sheets, devouring the grass. In the blink of an eye they had wreaked havoc, leaving as a black cloud.

The sun and the warmth returned, but the devastation was horrible. There was no colour left in our garden. The tobacco plants had been ruined. The tree, whose leaves had once been reflected in the marlies' water tank shimmering in the night breeze, remained now guarding the tank like a living skeleton. Not a single leaf remained. Even the trunk had white scars where the locusts had nibbled the bark. The white scented jasmine that had reached to my bathroom was crippled by the locusts, so that only a few strands of the climber remained. The marlies lifted the sheets, which had become shrouds for the demolished vegetation. Only the rocks remained untouched.

What of the locusts? Had they buried their dead? Not one of the guilty invaders remained. Ours was a pleasure garden, giving peace to the soul, but what of the farmers who depended on their rice crops to survive? The locusts were no respecters of persons. But my child's mind reasoned that they too had to survive. I wondered how they could ever have any normal family life with such a speedy existence. When did they marry and have children? How did a baby locust come into the world? Who were their predators? They must have had them as the world is so designed. Happily our only tree survived the horror of having its leafy clothing eaten.

When our animals were allowed back into the garden they couldn't understand where their tasty grassy morsels had gone. The dogs immediately rushed around the now-leafless tree and bushes re-establishing their boundaries with their pee. The devastation also affected the caged birds who could no longer feed on the grass: not a single blade of grass remained.

As disasters do, the locust invasion had brought our extended family together and now we all had to help the marlies bring the garden back to life. The marlies planted another jasmine but alas, it never reached my bathroom window while The Ridge was still our home. Three weeks after the locust invasion the older marlie experienced excruciating pain in his right index finger. Our doctor, Colonel Emerson, diagnosed the problem as a whitlow and said the marlie must have time off. A whitlow is very painful and similar to a boil. There is no reason why a whitlow should appear, but it is more likely to happen when the sufferer is run down and under stress. My mother was convinced it was the result of worry brought on by the locusts – an unexpected after-effect of the locust invasion.

Clothes Make the Man – Sometimes

When my mother was dying she asked me to please look after Pa and especially to take care that his clothes were always clean and his shoes repaired. My mother knew that this was no small assignment. For many years in India I had helped her to carry it out.

"Wendy, your Pa needs a new suit made. Please go with Prague and meet your father after his work. Make a detour to Nawab Din. I have telephoned Nawab Din and he is expecting him. I will also tell Prague."

"But Mummy," I replied, "Prague does not drive, Daddy always drives."

"Never mind. Prague can be very helpful and offer to drive Pa to Nawab Din. Of course your Pa will refuse but that is when you can persuade him. Remind him that Nawab Din escaped the Quetta earthquake and is trying to get his business established."

So it was that Prague, our chauffeur, and I set off to meet my Pa at the courthouse. When we arrived I moved to the back of the car so that Pa could sit beside Prague in the passenger seat.

Pa bounced down the steps of the courthouse prepared to take the wheel.

"Why are you in the driver's seat?" he demanded of Prague.

I immediately leapt to Prague's defence and explained that my mother wanted Prague to drive Pa to our tailor, Nawab Din, to be measured for a new suit.

"Move over, Prague," Pa said, "I know the way to Nawab Din."

He started the car and when he did not take the road to Nawab Din Prague tentatively reminded him, "The Memsahib wants you to stop at Nawab Din to be measured for a new suit."

"No, no, not today." Pa replied.

Prague continued in a gentle monologue: "But the Memsahib will be upset with me."

"No, no," Pa replied. "Perhaps tomorrow?"

Then I chirped in. "But Nawab Din is expecting you."

At that moment a donkey cart came into the path of the car and Pa had to slow down.

"Now Sir," Prague continued, "if you take the next turning on the right you will be at Nawab Din's." Pa would not agree. "Tomorrow," he said. "I have had a trying day in court. I need a walk and some fresh air."

When we arrived home my mother was surprised that we were early. She quickly learned that we had not persuaded Pa to go to Nawab Din's. My mother had to telephone Nawab Din and ask if she could rebook the same time but for the next day. Nawab Din graciously agreed.

The next day came but both Prague and I felt more relaxed. With luck, Pa would have had a less-strenuous day in court. Again Pa came speeding down the stairs and jumped into the driver's seat. We started off and again an obstruction, this time a camel cart, slowed us down. This gave Prague his cue. "Remember Sahib, a visit to Nawab Din scheduled yesterday is postponed for today."

"Prague, you are as good as my secretary." Pa admired his persistence and courage so it was agreed and he drove to Nawab Din's. Nawab Din was a man of no nonsense. Pa, "a burra sahib," needed "a burra tailor" and he was the only tailor to make Pa a suit. The tape measure came quickly into action – too quickly for Pa who insisted on knowing the size of Nawab Din's chest. So it was with much patience and perseverance that Nawab Din eventually got all the measurements he required. Pa and Nawab Din selected the material they liked and I took a sample for my mother's approval. She and Pa would together make the final decision.

Surprisingly, Pa was still in a good mood when we greeted my mother. Alas, there had to be a follow-up appointment. Miraculously it took place and the conversation drifted onto the Quetta earthquake and how it had affected Nawab Din's family.

It was the same when Pa's clothes needed cleaning. He maintained that dry cleaning took the nap out and spoilt the texture of the tweed. My mother kept a duplicate of every suit Pa owned so that he never noticed when one had to be cleaned. I had to sneak the suit out of the house without Pa's knowledge, bring it back the same day if possible, and return it to his wardrobe. Shoe repairs required the same stealth. It was no easy task attending to Pa's clothes.

My favourite piece in Pa's collection of brass. When closed, it resembled a thick candlestick. If you turned a revolving piece at the bottom, the top opened, releasing the brass petals of the lotus. Inside the lotus was a brass figure of a beautiful girl, the lotus dancer.

My Mother's Secret Admirer

My mother loved to play the piano and she had many musical admirers.

One admirer was very different. He had eight legs. Whenever mother played her repertoire of Chopin waltzes, mysteriously from the wooden beam in the ceiling a spider, Horatio, would perform his circus act. He did not weave a web but produced from his spinneret a long silken thread. His manners were superior to any human's. He lowered himself to twelve inches above my mother's hands. He stayed motionless, enjoying the music and, it has been suggested, the vibrations created by her playing. She played on, knowing that Horatio would not take the liberty of dropping on her hand. He may have been tempted but he kept his distance. If the silken thread weakened he ran up it, strengthened it, and returned to his favourite position one foot above her hands.

I never knew of Horatio's love of music until one day my mother asked me to sit still and listen. I willingly obeyed and only then did I realize I was not the only one listening with pleasure to her playing. I knew when the last movement was coming to an end and amazingly so did Horatio. He did not wait to give her applause but safely ascended his thread back to his home above the beam in the ceiling.

My mother did not play the piano at any set time, only when time permitted. Horatio, however, at the sound of the first note, was always there, descending on his silken thread unseen by some of my mother's other musical friends. His unobtrusive ways were loved by my mother.

Stella and Sandspit

When Pa lived in Bombay he belonged to the exclusive Bombay yacht club and sailed a yacht called *Sheba*, his pride and joy. The sea not only provided pleasure, it made it possible for him to keep healthy in a climate that

Stella decked in flags for a regatta. Behind her in the harbour are historic dhows from the Persian Gulf.

Stella, Pa's yacht, in Karachi harbour.

bred dysentery, malaria, cholera, and typhoid. The sea and sailing in Bombay's harbour gave newcomers a way of leaving the hot and noisy city behind. Pa would ask the secretary of the yacht club if there was anyone who wanted to sail. He offered two places on *Sheba*, and they were always quickly filled.

Some of the members were not accustomed to sailing on a choppy sea. According to the secretary who heard it from Pa's guests, the moment the sea was most choppy Pa would offer them sardine sandwiches. The large chunky sandwiches were the last thing the guests wanted. They learned to slide the slippery fish skilfully over the side of the yacht while munching the brown bread. Pa never knew, although he wondered why the seagulls, diving alongside the yacht to retrieve the discarded sardines, suddenly squawked with delight.

In Karachi Pa had a different boat, *Stella*. With Kassim and Dowd, the two tindals (crew), we often raced in *Stella*. Kassim always wanted to take risks and I remember on one occasion we either had to sail in front of a large liner or go about and lose our lead in the race. Kassim urged Pa to cross in front of the liner. He believed that we would be no worse off if we had to go about now as later. Our tiny sailing boat was dwarfed by the large liner, but the wind filled our sails and we went boldly across her bows. The risks involved in such a daredevil manoeuvre were many – the wind could suddenly drop and we would be becalmed under the prow of the liner. The liner sounded its warning bell twice but we safely crossed its path so no third bell was necessary. All the other yachts had been blanketed by the liner and we crossed the finishing line way ahead. Kassim was delighted.

Kassim and Dowd with *Stella* at Sandspit Beach, near Karachi.

Another time when we were racing I had been allowed to bring my great friend Barbara Mackenzie with me, but alas our course took us way out of the entrance of Karachi harbour. Barbara was sick over the side of the yacht and Pa, as well as holding the tiller and guiding the yacht, held on to her ankles as the sea was choppy and he had to prevent her from falling overboard. Despite this handicap we were again the first over the finishing line, though Barbara was not anxious to come racing with us again. On another occasion we jumped the gun at the start and had to turn back to the starting line, while the other yachts were in full sail. We managed to make up lost time and overtook one of Pa's friends, who called for a tow rope so that we could pull him along. Another yacht was taking on water so we lent them a bucket to speed up their bailing. Racing was always exciting.

We would often see the seaplanes landing. They were like gigantic birds and when their propellers were visible, they reminded me of the antennae on a butterfly. The floats on the base of the seaplane were like waterskis with the excited white surf dancing over them.

We often sailed *Stella* to Sandspit, a beach outside of Karachi, where we had a beach hut. We all loved going to Sandspit and brought with us a tiffin basket that contained a delicious picnic: sausage rolls made by our cook, and fruit complete with skin that could be peeled to avoid any risk of dysentery. Lewis came with us, and he would brew our tea. He filled the kettle with bottled water from home. It would soon boil on the kerosene burner. On one occasion when my mother poured the tea the milk curdled. None of us had any idea what was wrong and so we had our tea without milk. Then we heard Lewis laughing, which was most unusual for such a serious fellow. He had bravely tasted the water without boiling it. The water tasted of lemonade (homemade and delicious), which he had been boiling instead of the bottled water.

Pa wore a one-piece bathing costume, which was perfectly acceptable in those days as fashion did not dictate the use of bathing trunks. He swam sidestroke for hours following the flow of the waves, becoming a speck on the horizon. He stayed in the sea longer than any of us. My mother swam calmly and floated with ease. She said the only prize she won in athletics at her school was for floating on her back. However, she won other prizes in her musical studies. Joyce was an in-and-out swimmer and sunbather; Anne and I used to jump the waves and have fun.

The tiffin carriers en route to our hut at Sandspit.

One day Joyce, my sister, took Rex, her black cocker spaniel sailing with us to Sandspit. He stayed by her insistence on her lap all the way. He found the other yachts tantalizing and barked fiercely at them. The mud-fish that slithered on the mud flats provided him with great entertainment. When we arrived Rex ran on the sandy beach and paddled in the sea. He chased the seagulls but they were not particularly worried by him; they just flew away and landed behind him. Crabs that lay camouflaged in the sand were disturbed by him and made quickly for the sea. We saw Sandspit with different eyes. One very overweight Britisher who looked grotesque in his swimming trunks proved of great interest to Rex, who went running up to greet him. The man was not amused. He was one of the less-agreeable type of Britisher who spent his free time drinking at his club, constantly calling "Quoi hi" to attract the barman's attention, and unfortunately giving the British a bad reputation. We named this man the "Ark Royal" because when he went into the sea his great weight and size displaced the seawater as massively as Britain's largest aircraft carrier had done at its launching. Much to the consternation of the man, and my sister, Rex followed him into the sea. So great was Rex's attraction to this wallowing walrus that he even began to swim. Fortunately Rex could not dog paddle fast enough to keep up with the Ark Royal and returned at my sister's call to continue chasing the seagulls.

Sandspit was a nesting ground for turtles and there was a large turtle hole near our beach hut. Rex began sniffing and digging furiously, and we wondered if he would find turtle eggs, which were like ping-pong balls but with a finer surface. We helped him dig but we found no eggs. This turtle hole was where Pa had his afternoon nap. A large umbrella was placed over him so that he would not get sunstroke. My mother wondered whether the heat of his body might hatch any eggs that we had missed, but no baby turtles appeared after Pa's snooze.

On another occasion Pa was annoyed when two of our visitors, a young naval officer from England and a flirtatious friend of mine (who wore make-up), came with us to Sandspit and were also attracted to the turtle hole for their amours. I wonder now if the turtle ever knew the unusual uses made of her turtle hole.

———

Once when we went to Sandspit we arrived at high tide just as the fleet of small fishing boats was preparing to go to sea. "I would love to go out with the fishermen."

Although I thought it, I must have said it aloud. I believe Pa too wanted to go with the fishermen. But this was their livelihood and they would not turn their fishing excursion into a tourist attraction. Fishing was a serious business.

Pa mentioned to an elderly onlooker that his daughter would like to go out with a fisherman as a helper. The elderly man immediately called to Rashid, his grandson, and explained that a young missisahib wanted to go fishing with him. The poor grandson had to oblige. With great pleasure the elderly man beckoned to Pa, pointing out his grandson's boat. So it was that I had my excursion out to sea in a tiny boat like a canoe.

The grandson sat naked apart from a cotton loincloth, the fisherman's normal apparel. His slim brown body was a magnet for the sunshine. He perched on the folded fishing net so that he could see the waves breaking against the canoe.

When the sea was ruffled, signifying the presence of fish, he stopped paddling. Standing astride, he balanced the boat while lifting the folds of a net and throwing it out to sea. His throw was so expert that the net flattened like a large sheet. Then he pulled a string and the flattened sheet became a large balloon in the water encircling the tiny fish. He pulled the string tighter and then turned it around a small piece of wood. The magic balloon suddenly surfaced by his canoe. It was filled with hundreds of fish flashing like spilled mercury in the sunlight.

He hoisted the balloon, made silver by the leaping fish, into the boat. When he released the string the fish were suddenly landlocked in the canoe, slipping and sliding around my body and, to my horror, over my legs like an alive wobbly blancmange. The canoe became fuller with every balloon net he emptied into the boat. My legs were numbed by the feel of the slithering fish; I dared not move for fear of squashing one. This was Rashid's livelihood. Alas, I was taking fish space from him. What a relief when the sea lapped over the sides of the boat and the young fisherman realized that it was time to go back. As we neared the shore he nimbly jumped into the sea and pulled the canoe, heavy with his catch, onto the sand. I thanked him and he graciously filled a rusty can with six or seven jumping sardines for me to take back to my parents, a generous gift. No time for thanks as speedily his grandpa helped him empty his boat and he set out again to sea.

When my seven fish were truly dead Pa cooked them on an open fire. The taste was exotic, very different from any fish I have ever eaten since. No wonder seagulls love the sardine season.

Pa maintained the only civilised Americans he met were the couple who bought *Stella* when he left India. This couple I believe were Mr and Mrs Vance and he was the American consul. They kept in touch by letter with Pa on his retirement and gave him news of *Stella*'s progress at the regular Saturday races. One of the terms of sale was the continued employment of Kassim and Dowd, so Pa, having trained them, knew that *Stella* would continue to do well.

———

In the 1940s capital punishment by hanging was practised in India. Pa said he would never condemn a man to death unless he was so sure of his guilt that he would be willing to pull the rope of the noose himself. He took into account that murder provoked by hot temper was less reprehensible than premeditated murder.

Whenever we sailed to Sandspit our course took us past the Oyster Rocks, a steep-sided escarpment rising from the sea. In order to bring the yacht round the escarpment all hands had to tack efficiently to catch what little breeze there might be but the wind was completely blanketed by the rock and could not fill *Stella*'s sails. This demanded action and no sunbathing. Seagulls used the escarpment like flagpoles but they were barren rocks and held no appeal for the average person. Even the fishermen did not fish from those rocks.

Unhappily one day the Oyster Rocks became the scene of a sad and serious incident that caused much local concern. An Indian man took his pregnant wife for an outing to the rocks. He hired a local sailing boat that moored on one side of the rocks while he and his wife climbed up the other side. According to the husband they were nearing the top of the rock when his wife lost her footing and fell into the sea. Because he was leading the way he could not save her and the moored boat was out of sight. He scrambled down the rock surface and called for help to the man in the boat. They were able to retrieve her but could not revive her. When he returned to Karachi the police were notified and an investigation began into the circumstances surrounding the accident. The wife's overwrought parents were suspicious of her untimely death. The investigations revealed that the husband had taken out a life insurance policy on his wife four days before the accident. She was pregnant with their first child and in no condition to be on the Oyster Rocks. In due course the husband was charged with murder.

The case came before Pa and while we were on our Sunday outing the tindals, Kassim and Dowd, naturally were curious as to Pa's feelings regarding the case. All Pa would say was that there was no witness. We concentrated on keeping the sails full of the sea breezes as we were blanketed by the rocks. There was an eerie feeling on the yacht – to think that we were so close to what might have been the scene of a premeditated murder. This was only one of the many serious cases with which Pa had to deal.

What's in a Name?

In London, there was a large car-hire company called Godfrey Davis. When Pa, whose name was also Godfrey Davis, was home on leave and we were living in London, we constantly received telephone calls from people wishing to hire cars. Pa said he would have been a millionaire if he had been Godfrey Davis the car-hire owner and not simply Godfrey Davis. On one occasion a personal lady friend of Godfrey Davis the car man dialled our number by mistake. Pa answered the telephone and the lady recalled an intimate candlelight dinner they had had in Nice. Pa denied any knowledge of the occasion; at which she asked, "But you are Godfrey Davis?"

Pa admitted that he was indeed Godfrey Davis. "You cannot get out of it so easily," she replied.

While flattered that this unknown lady would think him the romantic type, he again denied that they had ever had a dinner together in the south of France, or anywhere else for that matter. Finally he realized that this was another call for Godfrey Davis, the car-hire owner. He jokingly relayed this telephone call to my mother, who, not wishing to miss an opportunity, suggested that Pa take her for a candlelight dinner in London. "Wishful thinking," Pa replied.

When Pa went on tour as a magistrate in the state of Sind he occasionally visited the local schools. His visits were a time of great celebration for the schoolchildren, who were granted a holiday from school work and given time to make garlands and welcoming banners. Songs of greeting to the Honourable Godfrey Davis became "Welicom, welicom to the Horrible Godfrey Davis" when sung by the children.

In 1941, while in India, Pa was named in the New Year Honour's list. Because it was wartime the investiture could not be performed at Buckingham Palace by King George VI; it was performed instead by the king's representative in India, the viceroy, Lord Linlithgow. This meant my parents had to go to Delhi, which was not agreeable to Pa because he hated the protocol involved.

On previous occasions Pa had objected to the time limits set on a conversation with the viceroy. He would be enjoying an interesting discussion with His Excellency when an officious aide would interrupt him to announce, "Your five minutes are up." Pa would reply, "We are having an interesting conversation and I am not moving on until we amicably end our discussion."

During a dinner at Viceregal Lodge Pa embarrassed the head bearer by demanding, "Please take this gold plate away and bring me a regular china plate that does not make the gravy curdle."

The viceroy had to allocate a special aide-de-camp to keep Pa in line.

In the weeks before the investiture Pa practised dropping on one knee while my mother knighted him with her parasol, saying, "Arise Sir Godfrey Davis." "I am not ready to arise," he replied. "I am going to meditate here for a few more minutes."

Pa thought he needed to practise because if he wobbled on his knee while being dubbed with the sword, he might lose his head.

This charade was enjoyed by the entire household. My mother did not escape the pleasures of being Lady Davis. In the same way that "honourable" was corrupted to "horrible" in Pa's previous title, Lady Davis affectionately became to Pa and me Lazy Daisy. Pa's rendering of "Daisy, Daisy Give Me Your Answer Do" was a constant reminder to my mother of her new status.

The local cinema had a royal box and the owner insisted that we as a family should use it when we attended a performance, otherwise it would remain empty and we should be taking seats that could be sold to others. This gave prestige to the theatre and its owner but not much pleasure to me, as I was not allowed to eat popcorn or ice-cream in this exalted seating.

It happened that the telephone number for the cinema was only one number different from our home number. While we were eating our evening meal, we frequently received telephone calls from people trying to book seats for the cinema. Pa would politely inform the callers that they had a wrong number. This would normally be the end of the telephone call, but on one occasion a lady refused to accept that she had a wrong number and requested to speak to the manager.

Pa informed her that there was no manager; this was the home of the chief judge of Sind. She replied, "Get off your perch. I want two seats for myself and my American boyfriend." Pa thought this was hilarious and responded by making animal noises into the telephone. From the dining room we could hear piglike snorts and donkey brays coming from Pa. Puzzled, my mother sent Fernandes, our head bearer, to take command of the situation and send Pa back to finish his dinner. Fernandes dealt with the lady on the telephone with far more tact and eloquence than Pa had shown.

Runaway Camel

I love camels. As a child it was a thrill to go to the London Zoo and have a camel ride. I was always allowed to give the camel a treat, a bunch of clover, upon my safe return at the end of my ride.

Among my father's collection of Indian brasses were two sets of camel bells. Bells were attached to a strong leather halter that should lie around a camel's neck. There was no way an eleven-year-old could lift them so I would tinkle the bells individually with a fork.

In 1944, while at home in Karachi, I witnessed a runaway camel dragging its cart in which sat the shocked driver holding the reins. The camel was terrified. Fear gives great strength and the usually obliging calm camel was out of his mind with fear – not of a terrorist, nor of another camel, but of a car that suffered an electric fault; its horn would not stop hooting. Cars were unusual at that time; the traffic consisted mainly of donkey carts and bicycles. This car was making a piercing hoot and I too found the sound frightening. My sympathies were with the camel. The more the driver pulled on the reins, the more fearful the camel became. Fortunately all the traffic, pedestrians, donkey carts, bicycles, cleared the way for the runaway camel. In modern times an emergency ambulance would be glad of such rapid clearance of the road.

This was a different scene to the normal threesome of camels walking rhythmically down the dusty road, one behind the other, with their loads of hay packed tightly in the shape of a fan on their backs, waving from side to side. Like a chorus line they mesmerized passersby; their charm was increased by the sound of their bells chiming musically to the rhythm of their stride.

The runaway camel had a leather halter of brass bells around his neck. These bells did not follow the normal gentle rhythm of a camel. They echoed the camel's fear and confusion.

The camel, its driver, and the cart were now out of sight, beyond earshot of the fearful sound of the piercing horn. Who knows what memories the hooting noise could have revived for this creature? I wondered where he had been before he became the property of his present owner. When did he first have a bit placed in his mouth? That must have been a painful experience: for camels, although they have a vicious bite that can dislocate a human arm from a shoulder, only have teeth on their bottom jaw. They have strong gums that grip like a vice, but their diet is lucerne and like cows they enjoy regurgitating and munching.

I hope the runaway camel was given a soothing feast of lucerne to recover from his introduction to the unsettling sound of a car's horn. By contrast his gentle farting did not disturb anyone. He was a loyal friend to his Muslim driver. I hope he was forgiven for his reaction to the non-stop hoot of the horn, so different from the sound of his own gentle camel bells.

Five

Kashmir

In the 1940s there was little air conditioning in India. In the same way that Parisians leave Paris in August, so people leave India's major cities during the three hot and stifling months of the monsoon season. Escaping from the heat of the plains for two weeks or longer in the hills made life bearable. From all over India people travelled to their nearest hill station, whether Simla, Nunital, Mussourie, or Kashmir.

During the hot weather in Sind, my mother, Anne, and I were fortunate to go to the cool Himalayan mountains of Kashmir. With us went our dogs Bunty and Rex but not Sally, our smooth-coated dachsund, who was inseparable from Pa. Sometimes we rented a houseboat on Dahl Lake near Srinagar, and sometimes we stayed at the boarding houses owned by Miss O'Connor, one in Srinagar and the other in Gulmarg. Pa was occasionally able to take two weeks' leave and join us.

I was lucky to have a father; many of my friends' fathers were prisoners of war. Heather Collins was one such friend. Her father had been
taken prisoner when Singapore fell to the Japanese. Heather came with us
to Kashmir one summer, leaving her mother, younger sister, and pet monkey at home in Karachi.

At Baramulla we left the bus that had successfully gurgled its way, after
a few stops to cool down, from Srinagar for a different form of travel: the
next part of the journey was to be taken by pony, the only form of transportation available. The syces stood with their ponies in two lines, one on
either side of us, and called increasingly loudly, "Bote ucha Memsahib,
memsahib" (Good pony, madam). Heather was a beautiful rider. She knew
immediately which pony she wanted, a lovely dapple grey. I felt that these
ponies were like the captives at an African slave market. The pressure,
noise, and persuasion that the syces exuded was overwhelming, encom-
passing us like a hot blanket. We were guided by Heather's syce and with
his assistance I chose Rani, the pony I later rode in the gymkhana at the
Presentation Convent School in Srinagar. My mother chose Bulbul, Anne
chose Raj, and Lewis had a very quiet staid pony only for the journey to
Gulmarg. The luggage was put on pack ponies and I felt for them as they
appeared overloaded. We set off to find the circular road that would take
us to Gulmarg. The syces walked behind us encouraging the ponies with
nasty flicks of their sticks. My mother insisted that we were in no hurry and
asked the syces not to flick our ponies. My mother did not have the figure
of Lady Louis Mountbatten, despite having the best ankles in India. She
was a considerable weight for her little mountain hill pony Bulbul. She
made it clear from the start that she was too heavy for Bulbul but the syce
insisted that the pony had carried heavier people than my mother.

The scenery was breathtaking as the mountain path went through the
pine forests. When there was a break in the trees the view of the snow-
capped Himalayas stretched endlessly to the far horizon – a vastness
greater than the Canadian Rockies. Our syces pointed out Nungaparbet

and suddenly I imagined that my syce was a sherpa who would one day take me up this Himalayan peak. Meanwhile we had enough to contend with as tigers frequented this type of habitat and the syces recommended that we keep going until we reached the green valley of Gulmarg. We each interpreted the magic of this ride in our own way. For my part I will always remember the birdsong. I could not see the birds but their notes were as clear as an operatic aria. The road lived up to its name and each circle took us higher up the mountains. After three hours we came to an open space in the pine trees and there below us was the valley of Gulmarg. The only signs of habitation were a scattering of log huts on the hillsides. One of these groups of huts was Miss O'Connor's Boarding House, our destination.

The descent was awkward for the ponies and not very comfortable for the riders. I saw my mother gently holding Bulbul's mane. It was soon over and we followed a narrow path by a stream into Gulmarg. We went through a gate that we later learned was the entrance to a practice area for the gymkhanas, polo players, and those learning golf. Tucked to the far right was a small wooden building, the local cinema, a favourite haunt of the syces and later of mine, Heather's, and my friends'. The films were always breaking down and when successfully repaired the whole audience yelled with delight. There were also two tennis courts by the far gate through which we left. We later played some very different tennis; being nine thousand feet high made tennis balls bounce three times higher than they usually did and running for the balls with minimum oxygen was another difference. This terrain gave our ponies pleasure. Perhaps they knew they would soon be having a well-deserved meal of oats and lucerne. Their thoughts were unknown to us. We and the syces were mightily surprised when they took off at a gallop, including Bulbul with my mother fortunately still holding her mane.

I found it a relief to be on flat terra firma. As I watched Heather riding with such enthusiasm, some of her confidence brushed off on me. To our delight our ponies, having had their private Derby, came to a dignified halt

Nearing the entrance to Miss O'Connor's Boarding House in Gulmarg, Kashmir.

at the end of the polo field. We waited for the red-faced syces to catch up with us. They too had been taken by surprise or else they would have led our ponies quietly across the field. The ponies nudged each other and had their own conversations. The air had intoxicated them. My mother was delighted with her adventure and complimented her syce on how well cared for Bulbul must be to carry her weight up the mountain and still have the energy to participate in their races.

We ascended a small hill and circumvented Nedous Hotel, which consisted of wooden cabins merging with the scenery. We later frequented the café at Nedous Hotel and had the most delicious sweet green raspberries that I have ever tasted. Down a small hill we rode and, crossing a stream, realized we were in the middle of a golf course with golf balls whizzing over our heads. One ball plopped into the stream we had safely crossed. Then up a narrow stony path to an open gate in a dilapidated wooden

An approach to Miss O'Connor's, Gulmarg. Note all the baby male calves, fodder for the snow leopards.

fence. This was the entrance to Miss O'Connor's Boarding House. There were many male baby calves with beautiful liquid brown eyes and black noses grazing on the grass. Our ponies ambled their way through them and did not disturb their munchings. We later learned that the male calves were not wanted by the herdsmen since Hindus were not permitted to kill them for meat. The maharajah of Kashmir was a Hindu. No one ate beef in his domain. These calves had found sanctuary on Miss O'Connor's property. Others were less fortunate. They were taken to the lower forests where they were easy prey for the hungry snow leopards.

The syces suggested that we stay mounted on our ponies as we could be in one of the outlying cabins. One syce offered to collect the cabin keys but my mother felt that etiquette demanded she meet Miss O'Connor or her deputy. After a momentous journey, moreover, she wanted to be welcomed. The syce gallantly helped her dismount from Bulbul and accompanied her

COMIC DOG SHOW & RACES

WILL BE HELD AT

Miss O'Connor's River View

on

SATURDAY 16th MAY 1942

AT 2·45 P.M.

IN AID OF

KASHMIR ANIMAL WELFARE ASSOCIATION

WITH 10 % TO WAR COMFORTS FUNDS.

EVENTS.

1. The smallest dog with longest tail. 2. Dog shown in best condition. 3. Dog able to do most tricks. 4. Dog with the most beautiful eyes. 5. Dog in fancy dress. 6. Child and dog in combining fancy dress. 7. Egg and Spoon race leading dog. 8. Race for small dogs. 9. Race for medium dogs. 10. Race for large dogs. 11. Open Race. 12. Handicap Race.

SIDE SHOWS.

Fun for all. Do Come.

BRING ALL DOGS & CHILDREN.

SHAPES & SIZES IMMATERIAL

Entries Close. 10th MAY.

Entry forms from :-

Mrs MACCULLOCH.
H.B. MARCH HARE.

Entrance Rs. 1/-   TEA Rs. 1/-

TROOPS & CHILDREN HALF PRICE.

K.M. Press Srinagar

A dog show and races held at Miss O'Connor's in Srinagar to raise money for animal welfare.

to the office. Happily our cabins were near the main dining room. We said goodbye to our ponies and syces. They wanted to come at 10:00 A.M. the next morning to take us for a recreational ride but my mother insisted that we all get a good sleep and suggested 3:00 P.M. This was not acceptable to the syces as this was their siesta time. A compromise was reached and the magic hour of 4:00 P.M. was decided on. The ponies and syces ate at 6:00, so we rode for almost two hours in that wonderful setting.

My sister Joyce had joined the WACI, or Women's Auxiliary Corps (India), and was serving in the Signals. When the opportunity arose she took her leaves with us in Kashmir. On one of these occasions we were staying at Miss O'Connor's Boarding House in Srinagar. During the war many of the armed forces personnel spent their leave in Kashmir, so young women of my sister's age had a hectic social life.

Leading up to the boarding house was an avenue of horse chestnut trees that Miss O'Connor had grown from conkers. One night I heard a horse-drawn garry arrive at the entrance to the boarding house and voices, a man and a woman, obviously saying their goodnights. As I listened I recognized my sister's voice. In the silence of the night I clearly heard her say, "Oh no, John, no John. Not in front of the chokidar!"

Chokidar is the official title of a night watchman. It is an important job in Indian households but not a popular one: it is unnatural to stay awake at night and sleep during the day when all one's friends and family are up and about. It is lonely and for the most part boring, except for the hourly ringing of a large resonating brass bell. So any small thing that happens is noted by the chokidar – and apparently, on this occasion, by everyone else as well.

To my sister's dismay, when she came into the dining room for breakfast the next morning all the guests, who were European and should have known better, sang teasingly in unison, "Oh no John, no John, no John, no … not in front of the chokidar."

Tea with a Difference

One summer our friends the Herman family rented a houseboat on Dahl Lake near the one my mother had rented. The Hermans lived near us in Mary Road, Karachi. They had two thoroughbred Great Danes that a friend had brought to their door during the monsoon when the dogs were puppies. The owner desperately needed to find a home for them. Petty and Tiny Herman's hearts melted. It was an awful night for the puppies to be out as the monsoon deluged down amidst thunder and lightning. Unlike the innkeeper in the Bible, the Hermans made room for the puppies in their home. The pups thrived and grew larger and larger to the dismay of their soft-hearted owners. The Hermans' two sons, Colin and Ben, had a great time training their puppies. Alas, Thunder died but Lightning survived all the hazards of being a puppy in India. A Great Dane is a most acceptable dog in India because his fine silky coat provides no hiding place for the dreaded tick.

The houseboats on Dahl Lake were elaborately furnished with grandfather clocks and they made a delightful home for the summer. On our houseboat we woke to a chorus of croaking frogs while kingfishers perched on the bow, their wings gleaming turquoise in the sunlight, waiting to spear any innocent fish that came temptingly near the surface; the

A shikara on Dahl Lake.

lotus plant with large leaves and the occasional lotus flower gave the lake the appearance of a floating garden. On part of the lake there were genuine floating gardens in which vegetables were grown. No wonder poets wrote odes to the lakes and their surroundings: "pale hands I hold beside the Shalimar."[13] The maharajah's summer palace was in view of our houseboat and the Shalimar Gardens surrounded his palace.[14] These gardens were built by the Moguls and in the 1940s were much visited by tourists. Local shopkeepers used canoes as floating stores from which to sell their wares and were constantly paddling to the houseboats; they were no ordinary salesmen.

Some of the canoes were a blaze of colourful flowers, others carried trunks of semiprecious stones, moss agate, sandstone, and lapis lazuli that the sellers wanted to display; others had all sorts of embroidered items from numnas (hand-embroidered rugs) to delicate nighties and underwear.

In the background there were the fishermen harpooning fish. It was in such an atmosphere that we were rowed in our own shikara from our houseboat to visit the Herman family for afternoon tea. We were navigated safely to the Hermans' and we did not upset the delicate balance of the shikara as we disembarked to the more secure houseboat. We were soon ensconced in comfortable chairs sipping tea from fine bone china teacups. Lightning the Great Dane, as part of the family, was naturally included in the tea party. All went well until he decided to visit us at the far end of the sitting area. As he walked elegantly between the small tea tables his tail flicked from side to side and with incredible precision and bad luck it caught between my mother's nose and her spectacles. With the metronome movement of Lightning's tail they were flung through the open window into the lake, never to be seen again. It all happened within seconds. Lightning was beautifully behaved and it was unfortunate that his tail had the unexpected ability to remove spectacles. Negotiating the descent from

Aunt Petty Herman's houseboat on Dahl Lake.

the houseboat into the shikara for the return journey could have been hazardous for other items such as shoes but we lost nothing more and gave my mother extra attention as she felt strange without her spectacles. Living on a houseboat had other consequences. We became adept at throwing our bowls of washing water into the lake and when we returned to life on land we had to control our desire to throw our used water out of the window.

Lukri and Sam

Sam was an Airedale with a thick woolly coat and he lived with his master, Lukri Wood, who was in the Wazuristan Scouts, a respected army regiment stationed then on the North West Frontier. Lukri means wood in

Hindustani and was a nickname given to anyone whose name was Wood. Sam accompanied his master when he went on leave to Gulmarg. That is where we met Lukri Wood and Sam. They used to go walking and Sam would come bouncing up to say a friendly hallo to our dogs Rex and Bunty. Lukri was also staying at Miss O'Connor's Boarding House and he would drop by and have a cup of tea with us while the dogs played on the grass outside.

Lukri's family were in Canada and of course he missed them, but after the war he planned a great reunion with lots of rejoicing. Meanwhile Gulmarg had its share of bored wives whose husbands were unable to stay for the three months that their wives spent in the hill station. These women were given nicknames. I remember a Calcutta Cobra, an Amorous Amritsar, and a Bewitching Bombay; we hoped our cups of tea with Lukri would keep him from these tempting females. When his leave ended he asked if we would take care of Sam so that his dog could have another month in cool Gulmarg. Of course we were delighted. The plan was that when our month was up and my mother returned to Karachi, she would take Sam as far as Rawalpindi where she would hand him over to Lukri's colleague. The colleague would be returning to the Northwest Frontier and so bring Sam to Lukri. If Lukri was drafted to Burma his friend would continue to care for Sam.

We had a wonderful month with Sam. He was the greatest help when we were bothered by salesmen. We were very vulnerable because we used to sit and read on our verandah and enjoy the fresh air. We were a sitting target. At first we were interested in seeing all the local wares and bought gifts for our friends, but there was a limit to our buying. We explained to the salesmen, "Not today thank you." When they persisted we used to say "JOW SHOO SAM," and Sam would growl fiercely and chase them away. Sam was elderly and his bark was definitely worse than his bite for his teeth were completely worn down. His food had to be minced as he was unable to chew it sufficiently to digest properly.

Lukri and Sam. Lukri was on leave from
the North West Frontier.

The war did not make it easy to keep in touch with friends in the armed
services. We lost touch with Lukri and Sam and have only photos and
memories of a time so long ago.

A Sari Is Not for Swimming

One summer the Bushby family came to Dahl Lake on leave from Karachi
where Mr Bushby worked for the public works department. They rented
a houseboat for a month while I was at school in Srinagar. Their two
daughters, Beryl and Susan, were my friends. One Saturday they treated

me to an outing on their houseboat. The trip was fun. We crossed the Jhelum River in a canoe and then rode in a tonga, the local taxi, and finally in a luxury shikara to their houseboat. A British tourist with a strange sense of humour had suggested names for the shikaras and houseboats and the Kashmiris, not being familiar with the English language, had readily accepted his suggestions, hoping that the British names would encourage other British tourists to rent them. However, houseboats named "Measely Morris," "Poxy Paul," and "Suffering Moses" were hardly conducive to business. The caption under the awning of our shikara read "No Fleas Found Here," which was a more comforting claim. The sun shone and the houseboats were like library books placed side by side on the shimmering lake. Positioned thus, more houseboats could be accommodated and all would have a view of the distant snow-capped Himalayan mountains. The shikara men paddled swiftly towards the Bushbys' houseboat and I felt as if we were Oxford rowing against Cambridge as they raced another shikara going in the same direction.

The parent Bushbys were sunbathing on the flat roof of the houseboat but their ayah, in a distinctive white sari, was awaiting our arrival. She watched as one of the crew on the boat caught the rope securing the shikara to the houseboat. We safely left the shikara but as we entered the houseboat we heard a loud splash. To our dismay their ayah had fallen in the water. One end of her sari was caught on the narrow deck of the houseboat and trailed behind her like the large white sail of a capsized boat. Beryl grasped the end of the sari and began to pull on it. She hoped this would pull her ayah closer to the houseboat but alas, the yards and yards of sari unwound and the ayah was getting thinner and thinner and more and more anxious that she would be exposed naked to all of us.

Fortunately the shikara we came in was still moored, and the men paddled to her and pulled her soaking wet onto the cushioned passenger seat. She was soon safely aboard the houseboat. A slight misfooting had caused the accident. The shikara men were quick to demand rupees for their rescue mission and in truth they would lose precious customers while the shikara seats dried. The extra washing might ensure that there were indeed no fleas as the caption on the awning promised. The Bushbys' ayah recovered from her embarrassing experience but we had a hard time hiding our mirth. It was the yards and yards of sari and her being unwound that had completely baffled us. The yards of silk also kept her from drowning as she rolled over and over on the surface of the water. Even if she could swim it would have been difficult in a sari.

The Bushbys sent us out again in their shikara and we were very careful not to upset it. It was more fun to be in the small paddle boat than drinking tea on the sundeck of the houseboat in the warmth of the sun's

A fisherman on Dahl Lake.

rays. The ayah's adventure made me think of when we rented a houseboat and the dogs, Bunty and Rex, fell in, but they loved swimming and we were always happy to bring them back on board. We then had a wetting as they shook themselves before we could dry them with a towel.

The Bushbys took me back to the convent school. On the way we stopped on the bank of the river to visit Lala Sheik's fudge shop. I bought treats for the other boarders and gave a bag of fudge to Susan and Beryl to eat on their way home, but they could not resist the fudge and ate it on the canoe ride across the Jhelum River to the school.

Living on a houseboat is fun in the summer but quite a different experience in winter. During the cold months the convent school was inadequately heated and it was very hard to stay warm. I had terrible chilblains and the nuns treated them by applying raw onion and then bandaging my hands. I could hardly hold a pencil, which was a problem especially as I was working towards my Cambridge school leaving certificate.[15] It was then that my mother rented the houseboat on the Jhelum River within walking distance of the school so that I could live with her in comparative warmth. That winter the snow fell abundantly on the flat sunroof and the boat nearly sank under the weight. Only the speedy shovelling of our bearer Ahmed and a friend allowed the houseboat to regain its natural buoyancy so that the Jhelum no longer lapped at our windows.

A Terrible Mishap

While I was a boarder at the convent school in Srinagar, I successfully adapted to a different way of life but it took time for my stomach to accept the constant diet of dal and rice. The novelty soon wore off. After I had been at the school for a year my parents became concerned that I was not eating properly. They decided that I should stay with my mother and sister at the Kalaw Hotel during their two weeks of summer holiday. The

Looking at the Jhelum River from the Third Bridge approaching Srinagar.

hotel was a few minutes' walk from the convent school. The idea was that I should stay on at the school as a day girl, as I later did again during my winter on the Jhelum, and live at the Kalaw under the care of the owners, Mr and Mrs Sisson. Kalaw was named after the hill station in Burma where the Sissons had had their previous hotel. They were fortunate to have escaped with their lives when the Japanese overran that country. They dreamed, however, of returning to Burma. They had buried their silver deep in the soil of the neighbouring hills and wondered whether they would find it when they returned.

For me it was bliss having my mother with me and staying in the hotel, which was like a private house. My mother was expecting to meet friends, the Boltons, in Srinagar, who were coming from Bombay. Jerry Bolton was at the beginning of his career with the ICS. His petite wife, Barbara, was pregnant with their third child. Their three- and five-year-old daughters were coming with them. My mother had not seen them for two years, so it was to be a happy reunion. I remember I had been tucked up in bed for the night and my mother was reading to me when there was a knock at the door. Mrs Sisson came in with a telegram for my mother.

Terrible news: Mrs Bolton was in hospital and her family drowned. What had happened? Mrs Sisson realized that my mother had received a horrendous shock and needed a brandy. My mother learned later that Jerry Bolton had not wanted to disturb his young family by staying overnight at a daak bungalow en route to Srinagar, as was the custom. The taxi driver was tired and must have been relieved to reach the outskirts of Srinagar safely. Dusk had fallen, the light was poor. He thought he had taken the turning over the Third Bridge but had mistakingly taken a small turning that led down steps to the Jhelum River. It was easy to make such a terrible blunder after driving all the way from Rawalpindi in one day.

Barbara, Jerry's wife, had been sitting in front with the driver. Jerry thought the front seat would be more comfortable for the long journey. As the car sped down the steps to the river he realized what was happening and leaned forward to push his wife through the open window. Within seconds the car had been swept into the Jhelum. Barbara was pulled from the icy mountain water by Kashmiris who had watched in horror as the car plunged into the river. The shock could have killed her, but my mother believed that because Barbara was pregnant, she had the will to keep alive for the sake of the unborn baby. She was taken to the hospital in the nearest available vehicle, a horse-drawn garry.

After drinking the brandy, my mother left immediately with Mrs Sisson to visit Barbara in the hospital. Mrs Sisson had ordered a garry and they too had to cross the Third Bridge by the same route the Boltons had attempted. This must have been nerve-wracking as it was even darker by this time and the street lighting was minimal.

My mother never discussed her visit with Barbara. She told me that the contents of the Boltons' sunken taxi, when retrieved, would be brought to my room. This happened the next day. It was a very sad sight: the child's wet knitting, a cotton picture book, a much-loved teddy bear with the black silk nose worn from being kissed so often, and two dolls whose eyes would not close; they were full of water and tears flowed profusely as if they recognized the loss of their beloved owners. I emptied the dolls of the water and their eyes immediately closed as if now they too could sleep with the children. My mother told me that, at the time of the accident, Jerry, with his two little girls, one holding her knitting and the other a cloth picture book, were seated peacefully in the back of the taxi. Alas, too peacefully: they were all dead, drowned within minutes of their destination. The driver in front was slumped over the wheel. Did he too leave a beloved family? What a hard and responsible job it was driving passengers from Rawalpindi to Srinagar – all those mountainous switchbacks, one after the other, meeting buses unexpectedly, passing impossible unless the taxi scraped up against the rocks on the side of the mountain. And even that was preferable to being on the outside with the sheer drop. I have often thought of those sheer drops when belaying on a mountain in the Canadian Rockies, but there at least one has the security of a rope.

My hotel room became a nursery. So many cuddly toys, a woolly dog like a wire-haired terrier, a puppet, Peter Rabbit with a carrot, a monkey with a forlorn wet face, a colouring book with only the first page completed. A pencil box with brand new crayons, and no one to play with them. My mother came to empty yet another child's suitcase. Then there was a knock at the door and a tall man entered. He wore brown trousers, a tweed jacket, and brown lace-up shoes. The two latter items of clothing always make me like the wearer.

My mother leapt to her feet. "Teddy!" she cried with relief. The man held her in his arms. I had never seen my mother in anyone's arms, not even Pa's. I realized that their distress was eased by sharing. Ted Perry was married to Barbara's sister Mary and he had come as quickly as he could to be with Barbara.

It took three days for all the children's toys to dry out. Mrs Sisson gave us some cardboard boxes and we packed the now dry toys lovingly, carefully. I never asked where they went. They were symbols of the children's spirits wanting to give pleasure to other children. The little children's suitcases took longer to dry. Ted stayed until Barbara was allowed to leave the hospital and then took her to his home in Bombay, where she was cared for lovingly by her sister Mary. Later the same year Barbara was blessed with a perfect baby girl. After the war she and her little girl returned to England. I heard news of them through Mary and Ted Perry who, like my family, had also retired to Kent in England. Barbara and her daughter lived in Sussex. The daughter had a Shetland pony, perhaps making up for not having any brothers or sisters. When she grew up she attended a secretarial college. Her first employment was with Spike Milligan, whom she later married.[16] They both shared an Indian heritage, though where her father had served in the ICS, his had been in the British army in India.

Ahmed

None of our servants were happy away from their wives and children and our home, their employment in Karachi. One year Lewis came with us to Kashmir. He was employed to wait at table and to bring chota hazri to our

Lewis with a tame bulbul and our syce, on the verandah of our cabin at
Miss O'Connor's, Gulmarg.

rooms. At home he depended on the other servants and their wives for
company. In Srinagar and Gulmarg he had no one to chum around with
and was out of his milieu.

He was wonderfully helpful on the long train journey from Karachi to
Rawalpindi, but the car journey from 'Pindi to Srinagar was agony for
him as he became very car sick. At Miss O'Connor's his main job was
bringing buckets of hot water to the cabin for us to wash with since there
was no running water. He also had to get food from the kitchen for our
dogs. He objected to doing this because it was not what he was originally
hired to do. He associated anything involved with the dogs as below his
status. The servants' accommodation was not of the same quality as at our
home in Karachi. Lewis never complained, but even in the train going
back to Karachi he had a mishap. He was very sporting about it at the
time. He was sleeping upright in the railway carriage. The rest of us were
reading. Unfortunately Lewis was sleeping with his mouth open. On the

Left: Somewhat nervously I am holding a kestrel that had been orphaned and reared from a baby. Right: A magnificent falcon with a magnificent trainer, far more confident than I with my kestrel.

luggage rack above him some strawberry jam was leaking from the tiffin basket. As he snored drops fell into his open mouth. One particularly large glob arrested him in mid-snore and he woke up. To his surprise and horror he saw his suit spattered with red blobs. He was embarrassed because his suit jacket and trousers were badly marked. We were unaware of what had happened until he woke up. My mother tried unsuccessfully to sponge out the marks. At the time it seemed hugely funny but we sobered up when we realized that it would not have been so funny if the jam had stained our favourite dresses.

That year my parents decided that my mother should hire a bearer for the three months' stay in Kashmir. Miss O'Connor had put the word out with her staff that my mother wanted a bearer while in Srinagar and Gulmarg. One applicant appeared to be the answer to our needs. He came with excellent references from soldiers serving on the North West Frontier. As a batman to many officers he had learned to be independent and did not have to be reminded to clean the shoes routinely, care for the men's uniform, wash, iron, and shine the brass buttons on their uniforms. He would turn his hand to anything, even cooking. Of greatest importance to us was the fact that he had cared for the soldiers' pets including dogs and horses. My mother never questioned the validity of his unusual and glowing references although she tried to follow up on some of them. But it was wartime and the soldiers were constantly being transferred, so follow-up was well nigh impossible. Thus it was that Ahmed came on the scene.

Ahmed's appearance was hawklike, with high cheekbones, an aquiline nose, and bright beady eyes. His pale Kashmiri skin was beardless but bristly. As a Moslem he wore a white turban. Although he sported a few white hairs in his bushy eyebrows his stocky frame was animated and agile. Ahmed became a member of our extended family. He brought us hot water for washing, morning and evening. He was very punctual in the mornings and brought us all an early-morning cup of tea in bed. Then he sat discreetly on our verandah reading his Kashmiri paper. In the morning he always drew the curtains back in the sitting room so the sunlight would be flooding in when we entered the room. He took his leave in the morning and always checked with my mother to see what time she wanted him to return.

Ahmed found out that Miss O'Connor's cook made special biscuits for the dogs. A previous guest had asked that the cook make them according to her own recipe and this was now one of the services that Miss O'Connor offered to all her guests. Another family, the Pykes, friends of ours from Karachi, also had a dog who enjoyed these homemade dog biscuits.

It was the summer when my friend Heather was with us. She and I went on long rides in the morning and afternoon but we had to return for lunch to check in with my mother. One day my mother and Mrs Pyke, with her children, Kay, Owen, and Madeline, and their nanny, Evelyn, decided that we should go on an all-day picnic. Miss O'Connor gladly arranged picnic lunches for us. Perhaps she was glad to see the back of us. Our outing took us to Ningal Nula, a beautiful valley known for its alpine flowers.

We set off in high spirits with the dogs excited by the scents on the trail. Before long my mother, Mrs Pyke, the nannies, Anne and Evelyn, the syces and Ahmed, who had our tiffin, were left far behind. We, the young advance party, found the picnic spot but realized that we had no lunch. We were famished, having eaten an early breakfast. Owen remembered that his mother had given him a brown paper bag for the picnic. Owen burrowed into his knapsack and found it. To his great joy it contained crispy brown wholemeal biscuits. We ate them and they were delicious. We grudgingly shared them with our dogs, Bunty, Rex, and the Pykes' spaniel. Finally the rest of our party showed up. They thought they had one up on us because they had the food. We explained we had eaten the most delicious homemade biscuits and were not impatient for lunch. My mother was horrified. We had eaten the dog biscuits. We thought it a great joke and survived with no disastrous consequences.

The syces were concerned that we had ridden the ponies too fast, but the ponies loved their gallop. The syces took off their saddles, wiped the sweat from their coats, gave them a good rub-down, and the ponies were soon munching the lush green grass. We were all very good on the way home – no galloping – and the ponies were not sweaty when we reached Miss O'Connor's. At the time we never thought it strange that Ahmed had come with us but not the Pykes' bearer. Later, we learned the reason.

One evening we heard raucous voices coming from outside the dining room. Several of the staff had gathered around Ahmed and the Pykes' bearer, who were shouting and gesticulating at each other. Miss O'Connor appeared and we thought she would quell the noise, but her appearance did not deter their argumentative behaviour. She compelled Ahmed to come to my mother and the Pykes' bearer to go to Mrs Pyke. Ahmed explained that his dignity had been hurt but my mother rightly thought this was developing into an ongoing feud. Miss O'Connor confirmed this and said it had happened before:

"This has to stop," she said. "It is disrupting to my staff because they are taking sides."

Ahmed was summoned to our cabin and my mother discreetly spoke with him. Evidently he was difficult to calm and my mother was fearful that he would have a stroke. Finally he departed, not so cock-a-hoop, and my mother hoped that this would be the end of the feud. At breakfast the next morning she spoke with Mrs Pyke about the incident. Mrs Pyke was of the opinion that it was Ahmed's aggressive behaviour that had caused the problem. My mother suggested it was merely a clash of personalities and she was determined that the bearers' disagreement would not affect our friendship with the Pykes.

I inadvertently made matters worse. When Ahmed brought us our hot water each morning and evening, we poured it into a china bowl and proceeded to strip-wash with a cloth. The dirty water we simply threw out the bathroom door onto the welcoming grass outside. Behind all the cabins were paths, shortcuts to the other cabins. Unfortunately, walking along this path at the very moment I opened the bathroom door to throw out my used water was the Pykes' bearer. I soaked his trousers and he was naturally shocked and annoyed. I apologized and explained that it was impossible to open the door and check that no one was coming while holding a basin of water. He too should have been alerted to the six o'clock wash time. The incident put me in Mrs Pyke's bad books and she was sure I was in cahoots with Ahmed. Needless to say, Ahmed was delighted at the mishap to the other bearer's trousers.

One day we slept late in the cabin. Our usual waking time was 7:00 A.M. At 7:30 we woke to find no hot water, no tea, and no drawn curtains. No Ahmed. We did not mind missing a wash and early-morning tea but where was Ahmed? None of the staff in the dining room were forthcoming. If they knew they were silent. After breakfast we went back to the cabin to find Ahmed in handcuffs with a policeman standing on either side of him. What had happened? The policeman explained that Ahmed had been walking across the polo field at 5:00 A.M. with a tin trunk on his head. They were suspicious and demanded to know what was in the small trunk. When they opened it they were surprised by the contents. They now opened it for my mother. To her amazement there were the reading glasses that she had mislaid, a ring that she treasured, her fountain pen for which we all, including Ahmed, had been searching. My mother had even offered a reward to anyone who found her pen. Various other items including some earrings and Rex's lead were also in the trunk.

Nothing could subdue Ahmed. He had a reason for everything. The policemen were relieved that my mother could identify the items and Ahmed had to go to prison. The policemen stated that after two weeks if my mother wanted Ahmed back in her service she would be responsible for his behaviour. My mother was convinced that this would teach Ahmed a lesson and that he would never behave like a magpie again. She wished she could discuss the matter with Pa but there was no telephone and letters took so long. Mrs Pyke was shocked that my mother would even consider taking him back. Miss O'Connor was not at all fazed by the episode; in fact she was relieved that the Pykes' bearer would have plenty to talk about. Now there would be no one for him to have raucous arguments with. Miss O'Connor kindly made arrangements for one of her bearers to help us for the two weeks that Ahmed was out of commission. My mother thought that the Pykes' bearer had informed the police of Ahmed's impending departure and felt she should be grateful to him. However, her loyalty to Ahmed superceded the rights and wrongs of the situation.

Ahmed returned after his imprisonment not at all chastened. My mother wondered whether he had been in prison before for petty thieving. He considered himself a hero; for how many men had been handcuffed and imprisoned? Such was his exuberance that he took to washing my underwear. This was strictly the dhobi's domain but remembering that Ahmed had been an excellent batman we tried to go along with his whims. To my horror I saw all my underwear hanging on a line in my bathroom. He never asked. He took the liberty of handwashing it. Fortunately there was no outside washing-line or all the guests would have been entertained by my cotton panties blowing in the breeze.

When the time came for us to return to Karachi, Ahmed wanted to come with us. He explained that my mother needed someone to help her on the journey. He could take care of our luggage and see it safely from the pack ponies onto the bus to Srinagar. Then at Srinagar he could help my mother rent a suitable taxi, one with good tires for the long journey to Rawalpindi. Then at the daak bungalow where we would spend the night he could help with the bedmaking and prepare the evening meal. My mother realized that he would be a great help but wondered how he would be received by our servants in Karachi, who had been with my parents for so long. He did come with us to Karachi and was a help. It was providential because Pa was due to go on tour visiting the local courts. This involved his manservant sleeping rough and cooking. None of our servants wanted to leave their homes and so Ahmed was assigned to attend my father.

When on tour Pa had to travel by camel. On this occasion the camel driver inadvertently put Pa on a camel intended for carrying luggage. This meant that Pa had no comfortable padded saddle to sit on. When the driver proposed taking a shortcut Pa fervently agreed. Unfortunately, as is often the case, the shortcut turned out to be a longer journey than the regular route. Before Pa reached his destination he was in agony, gripping the pommel in an attempt to take the weight off his bottom.

Ahmed was in his element but caused some embarrassing moments for Pa. When he went to the market to buy food for the evening meal he informed all the store owners that his sahib was a burra (very important) sahib. Every chicken the store owner brought out Ahmed sent back, saying it was not big enough for his burra sahib. Finally he agreed on a large cock. The shopkeeper had to kill it and take the feathers off and he must have been amused at Ahmed's ignorance. When the cock was cooked the bird was so old and the meat so tough that Pa could not eat it. Ahmed, although he had to chew hard, enjoyed it while Pa was happy to have an alternative dinner of two fried eggs.

The following year the servants were relieved that Ahmed would be going to Kashmir with us and the dogs. When we crossed the border into Kashmir we went through customs. Kashmiris observed the Hindu law that forbids the killing of the cow, which is sacred. My luggage was searched and my bottle of sugar candy, called "Bulls' Eyes," was pounced on by the customs official. Ahmed explained that the bottle held only sweets, with no animal content. It certainly did not hold bulls' eyes as the label on the bottle indicated. "Bulls' Eyes" was a trade name – the sweets were black and white and looked like eyes. Ahmed explained they were intended for sucking to prevent car sickness and were necessary for me to take for the dramatic car ride that lay ahead. All his explanation and charisma could not save my candies from confiscation. As a result I was horribly sick and spent much of the journey with my head in a brown paper bag. This, combined with the heat, made an unpleasant journey for everyone.

═══════

After the war when we were all back in London Pa received a letter stating that Ahmed was coming to England for a holiday. He telephoned our house and we met him in Picaddily Circus where we all had a delicious curry. We said goodbye and I often wonder whether he became a freedom fighter for the Kashmiri cause. While the negotiations for partition, which neither Gandhi nor Pa agreed with, were in progress, Pa and his colleagues urged that Kashmir should be granted independence like Nepal.[17] Even after Pa's retirement he and a colleague wrote strongly worded letters to the *Times* recommending that Kashmir be given her independence. Sixty years have passed and the situation has magnified. I can still count to ten in Kashmiri. Ahmed was a good teacher.

Six

War and Home Collide

War within a War

The news that reached us in India in 1942 was depressing. Burma had fallen to the Japanese. It was expected that the Japanese would continue on to Assam where there were no fortifications, only tea plantations – and valuable oil wells. This was the home country of Rumer Godden who wrote so lovingly of this hilly part of the world in her novel *Kingfishers Catch Fire*. Allied ships that had escaped from Rangoon harbour, having been brutalized by Japanese bombs and torpedoes, limped into Karachi harbour. Some ships could be rehabilitated but others could only rest peacefully, providing parts to revitalize their sister ships.

The war in Burma was, I learned from Pa, a messy business. The Japanese were on the attack. Dorman Smith, the governor of Burma, had

behaved extraordinarily, leaving Rangoon in chaos while he himself escaped by ship, but leaving orders for the release of all mental patients and
prisoners. The dogs in the pound were also released and they joined patients and prisoners in searching for food in their new-found liberty.
Shops were pillaged. Everyone who could escape fled before the Japanese
onslaught. Our friends the Foucars, Tony, Fay, and their parents, put a
few possessions in their pillowcases and trekked out of Burma. Miraculously, they arrived in Calcutta looking so smart that people thought they
had come from the Calcutta races.

At Mrs Ancrum's school in Gulmarg there were many girls who had
lived in Burma. Helen McLarend had a good sense of humour but was
constantly questioned by Mrs Ancrum for not knowing her subject. Her
reply was that she had had to escape from Burma and had left all her
books there. June Elvers had also escaped from Burma. Her parents had
been in the forestry service. Judy Brown and the Morton boys all had
roots in Burma. So many of my friends' fathers were missing. At the convent school in Srinigar, Joan Bragg, whose father was a prisoner of war,
found relief in prayer. Her two brothers, Bobby and Teddy, were at Sheik
Bagh School in Srinagar so she was in touch at least with some members
of her family. These friends and their stories made us realize how close to
us in India the war had come.

In his book *Elephant Bill* Colonel Williams described how a team of
elephants escaped from Burma under the brave leadership of an elephant
named Bill.[18] Elephants worked in the famous Burma teak trade and their
trainers enabled them to escape from the Japanese. The Burmah Oil Company, the parent company of BP Oil, had a long history in Burma but now
the company's oil wells and refineries had to be blown up so that they
would not fall into enemy hands. The Sissons' Kalaw Hotel, which was a
refuge from the sweltering hot Rangoon summer, also had to be aban-
doned. More soldiers died from malaria and dysentery than from war
wounds. Wingate leading his Chindits was the hero of the Burma cam-

paign.[19] The Americans came in to support the British, Gurkhas, and Indian ground staff. The Japanese were tough fighters and superb guerrilla tacticians. They would make the sound of a wild animal or bird to draw Allied soldiers from their cover. Not only would the soldiers meet their death but they would unwittingly have shown that there were other soldiers in the area. The Japanese came within reach of the Assam border but with the Americans' help were held back.

The Americans were fascinated by those Burmese who wanted to sell them large cut rubies at what the Americans thought were very good prices even before they began bargaining. One GI generously bought and sent to his fiancée in the States a beautiful Burmese ruby to be made into a ring. She took it to a local jeweller to have it valued for insurance purposes and to her surprise and dismay was told that it was cut glass and definitely not a Burmese ruby. Heartbroken, she wrote to tell her fiancée that he had been cheated. It so happened that during this period the Americans had been having all the glass from the red rear lights stolen from their jeeps. It seemed strange that only the red lights were affected. Eventually someone put two and two together and realized that the Burmese were stealing the glass, cutting it up, and selling it back to the Americans as Burmese rubies. So ended the American romance with rubies, especially the Burmese variety.

Soldiers at Play

Our house in Karachi was surrounded by desert. At night water would seep up through the sand and then evaporate during the heat of the day. This left a film of white salt that transformed the desert from gold to white like an arctic hare changing its brown summer coat to winter white. On certain nights of the week truckloads of solders would come tumbling out of their vehicles and scamper down the rocky incline to the desert below.

The great attraction was the leather lozenge-shaped ball they brought with them, which they quickly started kicking. They speedily marked out a pitch with white paint and two poles at each end for the goals. Then it became a rough and tumble. Such excitement caused by the lozenge-shaped ball! Arms locked into their neighbours' arms, legs kicked desperately, then success, as the leather ball trickled out from behind someone's mud-covered legs. No words spoken but everyone knew the ball was away. No wonder the technical term for this procedure was a "scrum."

I could not believe the soldiers did not suffer broken fingers, so tightly did they hold their neighbours. Then like Tarzans let loose they raced across the pitch in hot pursuit of their prey, the rugby ball. The soldier who had the ball was swamped by his opponents as they piled onto him. Like a moving anthill they slowly disengaged themselves in response to the referee's piercing whistle.

Among these muddy bodies was one Brian Henderson, the hero of Joy Rossiter, a school colleague of mine. Our relationship brought an introduction to these strange men who came from another world and caused such pandemonium in the silent desert, normally the haunt of the early-morning salt gatherers. A long piercing whistle blew and with three cheers from either side, the game ended.

As rapidly as the soldiers arrived on the scene, so they disappeared; the only sign that they had been there was the churned-up desert sand – no garbage, no cigarette butts, no white salt. The soldiers were covered in sand that stuck to their bodies. I wondered how their bathwater would ever flow away as they were all caked in mud. Joy had been in the holy of holies – the barracks – and said they bathed in a great communal bathing pool. The bottom of the bathing pool filled with sludge and had to be dredged before the bath tiles could be seen. The soldiers created a natural mud bath like an alligator wallow. Maybe this added to the pleasure of their rugby games on the desert of Bath Island, Karachi, Sind.

Another pastime of the armed forces was to hit a small rubber ball against three walls with a racquet – squash, as I later learned this game is called. Like the proverbial "Mad Dogs and Englishmen" who, alone among creatures, "go out in the midday sun," I used to ride my bicycle at noon every Wednesday through the barracks to my music lesson at the home of one of the soldiers' wives. This took me past the soldiers playing squash. I was scared of bicycling past when they were involved in this activity. Firstly they only wore bathing trunks and their bodies had rivers of sweat running down them. The strength exerted in hitting the rubber ball made their muscles ripple and the ball ricochet, with a scary noise like gunshot, off the walls. Miraculously the sweating soldier was poised to hit the speeding ball as it descended to a manageable height. I had no reason to be scared as they were much more enamoured of the squash ball than of an immature schoolgirl riding a bicycle, even though I did get the occasional whistle, which thrilled me and made me feel on a par with my sister.

Joyce's Royal Air Force boyfriends flew low over our house, waving while my sister responded, much to the anger of Pa who considered it an unpatriotic waste of fuel. I hated the noise of the planes because it frightened my animals.

I had two slightly older friends, Rhonda and Pam, who were more worldly wise than I and interested in young handsome British soldiers. In the cool of the late afternoon we would go for bicycle rides with the intention of meeting some British soldiers. One day the soldiers appeared on bicycles only a little ahead of us; we followed them in a circle round the Sind Club but were unable to keep up with them. Imagine our surprise when they rode up behind us. They had lapped us and now demanded who was following whom. We gave all away by our red faces. Our bravado deserted us and at the moment of victory we turned tail and cycled to the safe but boring British Gymkhana Club.

My sister did not find the Gymkhana Club boring because she was taken dancing there by her boyfriends. One of them had a sense of fun and he would dance under the fan and make my sister's skirt whirl upwards, to her embarrassment and his amusement.

Various men and women of the American forces were invited to our house as they were friends of my sister's. We were prejudiced because the Americans were paid so much more than the British forces. The garry walla, or driver of the horse-drawn taxi, no longer stopped for the British soldiers because they knew the Americans would give them more money. It was known that one garry walla had been asked by an American how much the fare was and the driver had replied, "Four to two," meaning a maximum of four and a minimum two rupees, whereupon the American had handed over forty-two rupees to the garry walla's astonishment and delight.

One day at our house in Karachi the head boy was summoned by the puttiwalla as three American servicemen pulled up in a jeep at our front door. They wanted to know if a blonde called Virginia lived there. The puttiwalla was baffled by their request and when he explained politely that this was the residence of the chief judge, they refused to go away, thinking that the puttiwalla was lying to them. In all probability they did not appreciate the meaning of chief judge and, showing no respect, rang the front doorbell again. This brought Fernandes, the head bearer, to the door. Pa heard the disturbance in the entrance but, not wanting to interfere, left it to his reliable staff. Finally Fernandes, looking very embarrassed, explained that there were three American soldiers looking for someone called Virginia. Pa in a jovial mood sallied forth to deal with the unwanted visitors. The GIs were forthright: they had met a delightful blonde called Virginia who had given them no address or telephone number. They had not thought it would be difficult to find her as Karachi was not a large city and blondes were a rarity. They had gone to one house where, they complained, they "were chased away by a dog as large as a pony." Pa giggled to himself at the thought of his friend, Tiny Herman, housing a blonde called Virginia. He thought of all his friends and acquaintances and truthfully could think of no blonde, and especially not one called Virginia. In all probability the lady had given a pseudonym and, having had her fun, decided that she had had enough of their company. Pa was tempted to have some fun with this search and to direct the Americans to the home of his friend General Hind, but he changed his mind because it could have caused a major incident with disastrous results. What were American servicemen doing driving an army jeep and using valuable army petrol looking for a blonde called Virginia? Pa curbed his humour and said he was unable to help them. They left disgruntled to continue their search. Later Pa telephoned Tiny Herman to ask if he had sent the Americans in their search for Virginia to our house. The answer was a peal of laughter – he had indeed! The puttiwalla and Fernandes chuckled at yet another "Americanism."

I frequently accompanied Anne and my mother to their volunteer work at the wartime cafeteria for the armed forces. I took cups of tea, scrambled eggs on toast and other requests to the tables. The atmosphere was busy and there was not much time to talk to anyone. The soldiers and airforce men were thin and wiry and they really appreciated their tea and toast when I took it to them. My sister was always bringing home servicemen for a meal and I thought how lovely it would be if I invited some of these men to a meal with my parents. I was so enthusiastic that I invited one table of four men to come home for dinner. They were delighted. The mistake I made was not to discuss it with my mother first. Of course she agreed to my suggestion. On the appointed evening they arrived in a garry at our house and were made welcome. They enjoyed their beer and crisps on the verandah and they were happy throwing old tennis balls for Rex and Bunty to retrieve. I thought of some lines from a poem:

We won't see Willie any more Mamie,
he came back again and again
but he won't be coming home any more.
No more summer chases in the garden ...[20]

If this had all been followed by a wholesome sandwich, it would have been a perfect evening for them. Unfortunately, the formality of a dinner party was not their scene. Fernandes announced dinner and we were all seated at the dining-room table. The soldiers took little food when the bearer went round with the serving bowls. The conversation waned. My mother asked after their families at home and they were not very forthcoming. Then the dessert arrived, which was spectacular. Our mistry had made my favourite, a fruit salad, smothered in rich cream, in a basket made of fine strands of treacle, served in cut-glass dessert bowls with small teaspoons on the side. The soldiers did not attempt to indulge but said they had eaten well. Pa insisted they have some cheese and crackers and with these they were familiar and enjoyed them. After dinner they wanted neither tea nor coffee and said they must get back to their barracks. They thanked us and said they looked forward to seeing us all again at the forces cafeteria. Prague drove them home. From this new experience I learned "chacun à son goût."

On one occasion my sister, with my parents' permission, invited two American army officers to dinner. They were oblivious of the formalities and Pa was highly critical of their total lack of table manners. Pa loved rice and on serving himself he always heaped his plate. Lewis, our bearer, would discreetly warn him that there were three more people to serve. Pa always took the hint and ate no more rice. Lewis could not tell the Americans "austy" (steady on), so they heaped their plates with food and proceeded to wolf it down, not stopping for any conversation. They enjoyed their coffee and before departing asked to meet our cook who had made such an excellent meal. My mother was delighted and thought they wanted to give him a generous gift. They departed with very full stomachs. Needless to say they were already overweight.

The next morning my mother met with our mistry to discuss the food for the following day. This was a daily occurrence as we had no fridge and our mistry went to the market every day. My mother was concerned because our mistry was not his usual contented self. She realized that something was bothering him. Upon asking what the problem was, he replied, "The American officers!" Instead of complimenting our cook they had offered him more money to work for them.

"What an insult!" our mistry said in disgust. He had long been part of our family and yet they thought they could bribe him away.

Supporting the War Effort

Pa always tried to help with the war effort in any way he could. He knew what an important role carrier pigeons had played in the First World War[21] and wondered whether they could be used again. He telephoned one of the senior army officials to discuss it. An appointment was made for three members of his staff, a major, a captain, and a sergeant, to visit Pa and prepare details of what would be involved. The sergeant had kept carrier pigeons in England and was the most knowledgeable. The pigeons would need appropriate accommodation and this would have to be designed and well built.

An easily assembled wooden lattice structure was built on to the stone room in which Pa already kept his own caged birds. The entire structure was lined with wire netting to keep the pigeons in and the snakes out. There was a small opening at the top and a landing stage for returning pigeons to enter. This opening led to a partitioned area where the message could be retrieved from the pigeon. Because the pigeons were not undergoing intensive training they needed a large area where they could keep their wings exercised. This area was designed so that when it was necessary to catch the pigeons for training, partitions could be put in place to make it easier to do so.

The midday sun was intense and the birds would need protection against direct sunlight. Then there was the job of feeding the pigeons regularly and cleaning their accommodation. Our sweeper could not be involved as she already had a full quota of work, but Pa was willing to give the pigeons fresh seed and water every day. He needed someone as a backup in case he was called away to Delhi or elsewhere. Precautions had to be taken against theft or the possibility that some inquisitive person might let the pigeons out by mistake. For their part the army representatives were enthusiastic because training the pigeons provided further experience for the soldiers. The tentative plan was that they would come up weekly and begin training the birds, but it was Pa's job to check the returning cage and tell the officer in charge when a pigeon had returned so that the message it carried could be decoded.

Building the pigeons' new home meant using part of the hedged area where our two gazelles, Harry and Harriet, exercised. Suddenly our compound was abuzz with army trucks carrying crates of carrier pigeons. The pigeons quickly adjusted to their new quarters, cooing, stomping, and exploring their domain. My mother was shocked at this pigeon invasion, knowing what the London pigeons did to Nelson's Column in Trafalgar Square. Nelson's Column had to be cleaned once a year. She wondered how our house would ever be purged of bird droppings. Pa assured her that these were different pigeons, but "Godfrey," my mother insisted, "they still make large droppings. That is their nature." Pa said that the carrier pigeons would only be outside their quarters when they were on training missions. Initially about ten pigeons would be taken to Clifton, fifteen miles away, where they would be let out of their mini-crates and, it was hoped, fly back to our home. Once back they would only be interested in food and water, which they knew were in their quarters; they would not want to cavort around our home dropping their droppings. My mother still had trepidations about the venture but I loved the pigeons and used to watch them for hours. What gave them their homing instinct? How would they help win the war? A dove helped Noah in the great flood. Maybe pigeons had inherited some of their cousins' genes. I longed to go out in the army trucks and watch the messages being attached to their leg rings before they were released to find their way home. I had to be content to wait with the soldier stationed at our house, timing their return. This was the first stage of their training before being promoted to the barracks to take up their official duties.

Once I was playing hopscotch at the bottom of our garden and a pigeon fell at my feet. It had dropped from the sky. I picked it up. The feathers were so soft and the pigeon was warm in my hands. I could not feel its heart beating or feel it breathing. I wanted so badly to warm it back to life. It happened to be a Sunday and Pa was home, so I took the pigeon to him and placed it gently in his cupped hands.

"Yes, it is dead. Poor thing. There are no signs of injury. I do not believe it was attacked by a hawk." Pa made a note of the ring number and telephoned his contact in the army.

There was no message in the pigeon's leg ring and the serial number did not match those of our carrier pigeons. Pa believed the army would be able to determine its origin and they were to send a soldier to collect it at the earliest opportunity. I found a shoebox and filled it with tissue paper, cotton wool, and a few mothballs to keep away unwanted insects. Pa gently laid the pigeon in the prepared box and Pa gave a blessing to the dead bird. Pa could not tell me if the pigeon was young or old. He remained in our hearts as one of the unknown heroes of the war.

Petrol was needed by the armed forces and although Pa had access to all that he wanted he decided that he should show some leadership and economize in the use of his car. To this end he ordered bikes for my mother and himself. Anne, Joyce, and I already had bicycles. My parents' bikes could not be bought locally and had to come from the Raleigh factory in England via Bombay. This took such a long time that Pa had forgotten they were coming until a large van drew up with two large crates. Mohammed, our puttiwalla, announced their arrival and there was much excited discussion as to what they contained.

For the next two hours the whole household was employed with strange tools, screwdrivers, saws, and hammers, ripping apart the crates to reveal the contents. To everyone's delight two magnificent gleaming bicycles were released from their wooden prisons to the freedom of the Davis household.

Pa was like a child on Christmas morning with his new toy. He had to try it immediately. Mohammed, straightfaced but with trepidation, held the bicycle while Pa mounted it and then gave a gentle push to set the bicycle in motion. Not to be outdone, my mother, with our hummel's assistance, mounted the saddle of her bicycle and followed closely behind Pa. We all watched in amazement as the two wobbled through the large wrought-iron gates onto the windswept sandy road outside our house. They rode successfully down a slight incline but my mother suddenly wobbled again as a snake slithered across her path. She was unable to regain her balance and fell off her bike on to the adjacent rocks. Pa, turning to see what had happened, also lost his balance and fell into the arms of a large cactus. We watched in shock as this drama unfolded. Our elegant puttiwalla sped to their rescue. Pa thought it was a big joke but my mother was grazed, though fortunately not bitten by the snake, the cause of the accident.

Our puttiwalla offered to hold Pa's cycle while he remounted but Pa insisted on pushing his bike up the hill accompanied by my mother, while

Mohammed pushed her bike. When the bedraggled party reached the house we understood Pa's reluctance to ride his bicycle. His rear end was liberally spiked with cactus thorns. Then the distress began again as Fernandes tried to remove the offending thorns, which had penetrated through Pa's trousers into his flesh. This turned out to be a time-consuming procedure in which everyone got involved. Jokes about porcupines were the order of the day much to Pa's chagrin. My poor mother's pride had suffered as well as her face, arms, and legs, which were badly grazed. Lewis was very attentive to her, bathing the wounds with warm water and applying iodine with cotton swabs to the broken skin.

The rest of us continued to deal with Pa's ludicrous situation. Even after all our efforts it was weeks before he could sit down without wincing. This put an immediate stop to his bike riding.

So it was that one slithering snake brought a temporary halt to my parents' attempt to help the war effort. A dog, however, gave Pa another opportunity, in its way.

There was a group of dogs in India known as pye-dogs. The word pye derives from the Hindi word for outsider. The dogs all had similar characteristics, beginning life as adorable puppies and growing into long, large, lanky, beige-coloured dogs, merging with the dusty sandy scenery. They had no owners and lived on the scraps they found, which were minimal. Occasionally the dogs were rounded up and taken to the home for unclaimed donkeys and cows that were usually old and of no further use to their owners. It would, in our time, be considered a home for aged animals. The home, then referred to as the pound, depended mainly on donations from religious groups that did not believe in killing animals. The dogs survived most diseases because they had smooth thin coats and they could easily rub off the dreaded ticks. They had velvety ears that dropped over their heads, protecting their inner ears from dust and other hazards. One such dog had found a hole in the road to Pa's court and proceeded to have her puppies and nurse them there. The traffic was heavy and the wheels of the camel carts, if the driver was not extremely cautious, could have harmed her. She nursed her puppies in the middle of this turmoil of donkey carts, horse-drawn taxis, and the occasional car. She seemed oblivious to all these dangers, intoxicated with the pleasure of nursing her tiny newborn family with their eyes as yet unopened. Pa discussed the situation with Prague, our driver, and it was agreed that Pa would call the head of the police force and ask him to put a policeman on duty to protect the dog. The policeman would direct traffic around the dog so the camel and donkey-cart drivers would have advance warning of the problem and could help avoid a traffic accident. While in some countries the matter would be solved by destroying the mother and her puppies, in India certain religious groups considered all life sacred. This was carried to such an extreme that in some sects, Indians would volunteer in shifts to be eaten by insects. Serving as bug food proved their equal respect for all life, however big or small, and was a paid public service. Pa and Prague were pleased when on their return journey from the court, they found a policeman on point duty protecting the innocent mother and her puppies.

Many of the British servicemen had a soft spot for these pye-dogs and fed and befriended them. When they returned to England many of them took a puppy home. There was a six-month quarantine period for the puppies when they reached England, which necessitated their being housed in an expensive kennel. When we visited our dogs, Bunty and Rex, while they were in quarantine, we watched these tiny pye-dog puppies grow as large as Great Danes. I am sure the servicemen had not foreseen their puppies growing to the size of ponies. What a shock for their families, having to make space in their terraced housing and provide food from their meager rations.

On one occasion, when Pa was travelling by train in India, he had a sleeper compartment that accommodated two persons. He had booked the bottom bunk, avoiding the problem of climbing a ladder to get to the top bunk. When Pa boarded the train at Karachi, he had the cabin to himself. Later in the day at Drig Road, a young army officer, accompanied by a Great Dane named Jason, shared Pa's compartment. The officer climbed up to his bunk and was soon snoring and sleeping soundly while his dog lay on the floor next to Pa. Poor Jason was panting from the heat. Pa gave him a bowl of water but the compartment had no air conditioning and the dog was miserable. Pa took an ice cube from his icebox, wrapped it in his large linen handkerchief, and placed it on Jason's forehead. The dog's panting lessened but as soon as the ice-cube melted he began panting again. Pa had to replace the ice cube with another from his icebox. Jason showed his gratitude by licking Pa's face. In order to escape the licks Pa covered his face with his sheet which made him even hotter. Whenever Jason started panting, Pa knew it was time to replace the ice cube. This procedure went on all night. At the first train stop at 8:00 A.M. the young officer descended, rested by an uninterrupted night of sleep, and left the railway carriage with Jason, completely ignorant of Pa's sleepless night, which had kept his dog alive.

Patch the bull terrier with Pa and a puppy. Patch escaped from his kennel early one morning and wandered into a neighbour's house unnoticed. The horrified lady of the house awoke to Patch licking her face.

During the war, we had many visitors at our home in Karachi. Among them were distinguished members of the armed forces en route to various military zones. General Auchinleck, returning from the North African desert where Montgomery was fighting Rommel, the Desert Fox,[22] was one such visitor who made a great impression on Pa. We were also visited by members of the legal profession travelling to and from the United Kingdom. My only contact with them was when I asked them to sign my much-treasured autograph book. On one occasion a retired judge, Sir Patrick Spens, jokingly asked if he should sign as Sir Patrick Spens High Court Judge, decayed. Not understanding the meaning of decayed I replied with enthusiasm, "Yes please." Pa was horrified by my faux pas but Sir Patrick merely chuckled and autographed my book with a quote from a famous ballad written about a Sir Patrick Spens, one of his predecessors.

At one point a contingent of Polish refugees in transit lived for a time under canvas on the outskirts of Karachi. The hot Sind desert and the gruelling sun made life unpleasant for them. So it was that Veronica, a Polish seamstress, came to spend the days with us. I tried to teach her English and she tried to teach me Polish. Nowadays both in Britain and Canada I have special Polish friends. I often wonder what happened to Veronica.

One day we had a welcome surprise telephone call from none other than Leslie Hard, whose taxi we used to rent in South Devon before we left for India. He was in Karachi serving with the RAF. Pa arranged for Prague, our driver, to bring Leslie home for dinner from his base at Drig Road. Leslie enjoyed the meal, especially since the food at the mess was awful. It was provided by local caterers who made large profits by supplying poor-quality produce. For the remainder of his stay in Karachi Leslie spent most of his off-duty time at our house.

In 1940 when my mother, Anne, and my sister and I arrived in Karachi from England, the governor of Sind was Sir Launcelot Graham. He was tall and distinguished with a lovely wife. When they went on tour they had a private train. In his retinue was their pet dachshund, George. The dachshund was another good breed for India because their short, smooth coats made it easy to find the ticks that gave dogs tick fever, which could kill them. On train journeys it was Sir Launcelot's practice to use the train stops to take his dog for a pee. Once while engaged in this the train left without him and his dog. Lady Graham was sleeping on the train and did not notice their absence.

Sir Launcelot found the stationmaster and explained that his private train had gone without him. The stationmaster was unimpressed by his story. Sir Launcelot was taken aback when the stationmaster did not immediately try to solve his problem.

"But I am Sir Launcelot Graham, the governor of Sind," said Sir Launcelot.

"And I am the shah of Persia," was the stationmaster's retort.

When Lady Graham awoke and realized that her husband and their dog were not with her, she reported their absence to her bearer, who reported to the guard, who then reported to the train driver. After some panic on the part of the driver, the train was put in reverse and two hours later an embarrassed Sir Launcelot was rescued from the platform.

By this time Sir Launcelot was in need of a rest stop as there had been no lavatory at the station. Sir Launcelot's tiny smooth-haired dachshund, which only came up to his feet, had almost caused a diplomatic incident.

We were all aware of Hitler's terrible trains in Europe taking Jews and others to concentration camps and gas chambers. I wondered why those rail lines were not targeted by the Allies.

The Mountbattens stayed for a few days in Karachi at Government House, where my parents attended a dinner party in their honour. Lord Louis, the new viceroy, had been sent by Mr Attlee, then Labour prime minister of Britain, to plan to effect independence for India within a ridiculously short time.[23] His predecessor, Lord Wavell, was known by the Indians, having served as an army officer with them. His grey hair represented knowledge and he was loved and respected, but the Labour gov-

Sir Launcelot and Lady Graham. Sir Launcelot was
governor of Sind.

ernment did not respect his ideas. Lord Louis was sent as a figurehead, a
colourful personality with no experience of Indian politics. He told Pa this
was the bloodiest assignment he had ever been involved in.

Sir Hugh Dow was the governor of Sind after Sir Launcelot Graham.
They were different in stature and personality which was only to be expected. Pa liked Sir Hugh, whom he found intelligent, down to earth, and
reliable. His wife was a small lady but always made her presence known.
At a formal dinner attended by the new viceroy and his wife, Lord Louis
helped himself to his favourite English Cheddar cheese. Pa heard Lady
Dow commenting that cheese was difficult to come by.

Years later, when I worked in a hospital in Edmonton and was asked to find vases for patients' flowers, I thought of Lady Dow. Hospitals are always busy places, but in India during the war they were more than usually understaffed and the staff overworked. In such a setting Lady Dow would appear with a bunch of prized daffodils, which were very rare in Karachi. She would demand a suitable single-stemmed vase so that each soldier could have a daffodil on his bedside table. The nurses had no such thing and generously gave her drinking glasses, which she promptly rejected. In desperation they gave her a urinal and to their amazement this fitted the bill. Fortunately they had extra urinals, so all the daffodils could be accommodated and Lady Dow's mission was successfully completed. No doubt the wounded were entertained and their urinals, though occupied by the flowers, were close at hand.

The "Quit India" Campaign

On 14 July 1942, taking advantage of Britain's weak position in the war, a working committee of Congress adopted a "Quit India" resolution the gist of which was that Indian leaders would support Britain in exchange for independence.[24] Large "Quit India" posters defaced the beautiful pink stone of the high court. Pa ordered that these be pulled down daily and recycled to help in the war effort. Did the Indians want the Japanese to replace the British? In Pa's court there were four other judges: Mr Western, who was British, and Mr Hatim Tyabji, Mr Charles Lobo, and Mr Desaar, who were Indian. They were being trained to take over his position on his retirement. They were concerned; of course India must be independent. The Indian judges were an integral part of the high court, which was held in high esteem by the whole of India. Law students came from all over the continent to observe the way justice was administered. Given time these Indian judges would have been capable of managing the judiciary.

Lord Wavell (Field Marshall Viscount Archibald P.), soldier and poet, much loved by his Indian troops and respected by all for his grey hair and wisdom. He was viceroy from June 1943 to March 1947. Pa was among the many who believed that Lord Wavell could have brought a united India to independence.

Top: The high court in Karachi. During the "Quit India" campaign the beautiful pink sandstone of the building was defaced by posters. Pa had them torn down each day and the paper recycled for the war effort.

Above: Pa with three of the judges he was training to take over the high court in Karachi upon his retirement.

The Quit India posters were followed by a cannon attack on the court. This was a surprise to the judiciary. Fortunately the perpetrators of the attack were not expert marksmen and the cannon balls exploded in an undeveloped part of Karachi where the military played soccer. This debacle caused a great deal of mirth and undermined the Quit India cause. Everyone realized that the attackers might try again and probably succeed: they would not want to be laughed at a second time. It was a disturbing period. The news from all fronts was full of Allied defeats. Most Indians showed enormous loyalty to the Allied cause but the minority dissidents increased the pressure with their Quit India signs.

Even my sheltered convent school had its agitators. Sheila Kapur, one of our best hockey players and my friend, stamped on the Union Jack and gave us all Congress flags. This was a disruption to the tolerance that usually prevailed at the school but it was very important to Sheila Kapur. I heard later that she married a senior army officer who was promoted to a general and held an important position in independent India.

In time the tide of battle in the world war thankfully turned in the Allies' favour. The Indian war within a war continued to a bloody conclusion. Lord Wavell, who would not agree to be party to an accelerated deadline for independence, had been replaced as viceroy by Lord Mountbatten. Mr Jinnah refused to give an inch in his demands for the creation of a separate Muslim state in Pakistan. Mr Nehru, equally stubborn, demanded that Kashmir not be made independent like Nepal.[25] Gandhi's dreams of having all political factions and religions represented in the Indian government as in Switzerland became an impossibility.

Seven

❦

Out of India

My mother and I returned to England in 1945 after the British had landed in France. We sailed on the *Magdapur* through the Mediterranean. On arriving in England I went to Roedean School, which had been evacuated to the Lake District but later returned to its original site in Brighton, Sussex. My sister Joyce was demobbed from the Indian army and returned by ship to England in 1946. She later married Michael Seys-Phillips whom she met in the British Territorial Army.

By the time my mother and I left India Anne was with another British family and returned with them to England. She spent her holidays with us.

In 1947 my father returned to England via New Zealand in order to visit my mother's sister and her husband. He had been asked to preside at the Nuremberg trials[26] in Germany after the war but he refused, because of his health and because my mother wanted a settled home in England, having always been parted either from her children or from her husband.

Once back in England, Pa was unbearably homesick for India. As a young man going to India with the enthusiasm and altruism of youth, he had happily devoted his life to the people and the justice system of that country. He continually said that after spending thirty years in India he should have been gassed on his return to England; he meant it. To lessen his despondency my mother, while they were living in London, wisely encouraged him to consider a new career. To this end he attended Seabrooks, an agricultural college in Chelmsford in the county of Essex where he learned fruit farming. Agriculture had always been a great love of his. After much searching my parents found a house, Beresfords, in Kent with land suitable for growing apples. Pa, with assistance, was happy planting apple trees and dreaming of an orchard. A nightmare interrupted these dreams: my mother became very ill. I remember Pa's telephone call to me in London.

"Your mother has been sick, and you must come home immediately."

I realized I would need permission to leave my work and give my employer time to find a replacement. A replacement for how long, I wondered. While I was deep in thought Pa continued, "Time is of the essence. You must come tomorrow."

He was sure they would understand at work. They did understand and the next afternoon I took the train from Victoria Station to Maidstone in Kent and a bus from there to our village, Boughton Monchelsea. In the end I was at home caring for my mother for two years. After many heartbreaking crises my mother died, far too young, in 1955. I then worked at Guy's Hospital in London as a medical secretary. My efforts at living and working in London during the week and returning to care for Pa at weekends were hopelessly inadequate.

I had a school friend, Jocelyn Emberton, whose father was a much-respected architect in London.[27] Tragically, his life was cut short by a fatal heart attack. After my mother's death I lived for a time with Pa in Kent. I tried to keep the house warm with interesting visitors and arranged for my friend Jocelyn and her widowed mother to visit us. Kathleen Emberton told Pa how her late husband had always insisted on living near bus stops which made her feel that she was married to the bus stops as much as to the man. Living on a bus route enabled her husband to commute to his office. The Embertons lived in Brighton and Mr Emberton took the train every day to London. Mrs Emberton said that whatever train carriage her husband travelled in the commuters read the *Times*. Not wishing to appear different he also bought the *Times*, but resting inside his copy was the *Cage and Aviary* paper, which he read surreptitiously. This amused Mrs Emberton: if it had been the *Cosmopolitan* of the day or some such juicy magazine it would have been worth camouflaging.

A few of my parents' friends visited Pa, but a brief visit over a cup of tea did not alleviate his intense loneliness. Mrs Hope, Mrs Macmillan Scott, and others did their best, visiting and listening to his tales of India. Those who were widowed said they had had one good man and that was sufficient; now they had adapted to living on their own. I believe it is so much harder when a man is left on his own.

Pa had a lady Australian pen friend. Their correspondence began over the rearing of Goldian finches and then widened to the rearing of mealworms and other insects. They had started writing when my mother was alive and my parents were still living in India. I loved seeing the beautiful Australian stamps that came on the envelopes. Fortunately no live specimens were sent in the post. I encouraged Pa to renew his correspondence with his pen friend, but now that my mother was gone he had lost enthusiasm for writing. He said that before he retired he had had no time to write, and now that he had retired he had not the spirit to do so.

Amidst all this turmoil I had kept in touch by letter with Ambalal Sarabhai, Pa's friend in Ahmedabad. Ambalal was sympathetic to Pa's constant loneliness. We received a cable from him: "Send Godfrey to us. He would be welcome."

The unbelievable had happened. A "welcome home" awaited Pa in

India. Pa, however, was extremely reticent about accepting Ambalal's invitation, sincere as it was. He had not travelled out of England since his return from India seven years earlier. He now had the responsibility of Beresfords with its young apple trees.

Then a letter came from Leena, one of Ambalal's daughters. She had been operating a school for young boys and girls out of her home. Now, with the advice of Madame Maria Montessori, Leena had designed and built a new school for the children and asked Pa if he would give the inaugural speech. Even so he was reluctant to go. Whenever I have a blinding headache it takes me back to those days of trying to persuade Pa to return to India.

During one such headache I took the dramatic step of purchasing a ticket from Liverpool to Bombay from the P&O Shipping Company. Pa would enjoy the sea journey. Ambalal had invited him for three months during the cold-weather season in Gujarat. The return journey could be booked later. I also bought two train tickets from Maidstone to Liverpool. I went with him and saw him safely on the ship. So, after many changes of mind, Pa finally went to India.

In Ambalal Sarabhai's home Pa had a spacious bedroom with a verandah and his own bathroom. He was never alone; arrangements were made for Ambalal's driver to take him every day to visit with those members of Ambalal's family who did not live in the family compound, and also to visit Leena's school. Pa became good friends with Ambalal's driver. On one outing the driver told him of the recent visit of Queen Elizabeth and Prince Philip and how he had had the honour of driving Their Royal Highnesses to Ambalal's daughter-in-law's dance academy.

The driver asked Pa if all English ladies were as deliciously scented as our English queen. Pa was taken aback by his innocent question. He replied in all honesty, "No," and the subject changed. However, Pa hoped that the queen was aware of this subtle appreciation from a valued member of the British Commonwealth.

All the while Pa was perfecting his speech for the opening of Shreyas, Leena's school. I had listened to the speech countless times before Pa's departure, but now in Leena he would have the best of critics to help him.

At last the great day arrived, and Pa gave his speech:

Now I've come to Shreyas which I think is one of the most wonderful schools in the world, founded and served by Leena behen[28] with love and wisdom and courage and devotion; and you must, I am sure, either teachers or pupils, be proud and happy to be associated with so fine a school. Whenever I came here during the past three months it seemed to me that here is a place where the spirit of Gandhi lives; here if he came, he would find a resting place; here are the children he loved, taught and cared for in the spirit of sacrifice for which he lived and for which he died. He would have seen in these grand and simple buildings their true nobility of purpose.

It is a noble purpose for which Shreyas works not only to educate but also to inspire with the love of service those who teach here and those who learn. It is you children who hold in your hands the future of your dear Motherland. You will be her leaders and her servants in the future. You will work to keep her great and noble – I will not say to make her great and noble – for great and noble and wonderful she has always been. But without love for your fellow men and women, and without the spirit of true service, new works however great, however long in the planning, will be but dust and ashes in the land.

You will remember there is play and exercise as well as work and study. The body is a temple or a shrine of the mind and spirit. You must keep your body fine and strong and clean so that it is a worthy habitation for the mind and spirit and here in Shreyas you have every opportunity to do so. You have a spacious campus and playing field and the still unsullied and unpolluted atmosphere of the countryside. Take, therefore, full advantage of the great opportunities offered to you; make Shreyas and your Motherland proud of you and this, I am sure you will all do.

God bless you all.

With this speech Pa led the opening ceremony of the school, a most a colourful and historic occasion.

During his stay in Gujarat Pa had his evening meal with Ambalal and his wife; he told me this gave all of them great pleasure. Every morning Pa was awakened by one of the staff bringing him "choti hajari" to his room and then later a full breakfast. Pa shared his breakfast first with a shy monkey that sat watching him on the verandah; later the monkey brought his partner and the partner brought his brother and so the number of visiting monkeys multiplied. After the monkeys had had a good feed and departed, Pa put the fruit that he had bought especially for the mynah birds on the verandah. He also bought birdseed for the wild finches. Even Ambalal's dazzling peacocks, which roamed the grounds, honoured Pa, making their presence known by their raucous screeches.

The sharing of his breakfast became a morning ritual looked forward to by Pa and his visiting menagerie. If he left his room on the second floor to visit Ambalal on the ground floor he found the birds waiting for him on his verandah. Pa returned to India three times to stay with the Sarabhai family in Gujarat. A guest who later had the room Pa had used at Ambalal's remarked that a great variety of animals and birds appeared daily at 8:45 A.M. They seemed expectant and he found it strange that they visited so regularly. Ambalal affectionately remarked, "They were Godfrey's family. He fed them daily."

I was not in Ahmedabad with Pa but he brought back such vivid descriptions they are imprinted on my memory forever.

One day when he was back in England Pa had a telephone call from a minister whom he had known in India. The minister was in London with his daughter who was going to the Royal College of Needlework and he wanted to come down with her to visit. I received a telephone call from Pa summoning me home to entertain the minister and his daughter. Pa now employed two men, Leslie and Roy Davis, to help in the orchard, and the a coincidence of their names led to many amusing incidents. Our housekeeper, Mildred, cared for Pa.

Alas, Mildred always resented my coming home and created ill feeling between me and Pa, which led to complications. Returning home was never easy. On this occasion I was needed to drive the car and take the minister and his daughter sightseeing in Kent. On the telephone I asked how Pa knew the minister.

"Oh, he came up before me on trial for murder, but there was insufficient evidence so he went free."

I did not relish the idea of having a man accused of murder staying in our house or driving him around for that matter. Then I realized any visitor whom Pa wanted to entertain was a distraction for him. I telephoned our great friends the Scovils, who lived nearby, and told them of my dilemma.

Judith immediately said, "I'll invite some friends in for sherry after church and tell my friends of your Pa's visitors so they will be prepared to entertain them."

I telephoned Pa to say we were all invited to the Scovils' after church and he promptly refused to go. He said I could go with the minister and his daughter. I could see problems ahead for the weekend. I wanted to use the minister as a lever to get Pa out of the house, making a change in the reclusive life that he unwillingly had to accept.

I took the train down from London to our nearest town, Maidstone, and arrived the night before the visitors, as Pa requested. I helped with the bedmaking and preparations and everyone had a common goal, so the atmosphere was happy. I went to the station to meet the minister and his daughter. They were easy to identify from the usual commuters. We met and were soon squeezed into the car. The minister was large and portly and his daughter, also heavy set, was delightful with continual smiles. I felt reassured that Pa would be charmed by her and would enjoy great camaraderie with the minister, who owned land and was a zemindar in his own right.

"Godfrey!"

The minister greeted Pa respectfully as Pa opened the front door. Mildred was quickly brought on the scene and the cold lunch we had discussed at great length was soon being enjoyed by all. The usual routine with visitors after lunch was for Pa to give them a tour of the orchard. When they returned the minister insisted on having a rest. This meant a siesta on his bed, so we all disappeared and recharged our batteries. I had a quick consultation with Pa and suggested that on Monday we all go to Canterbury for the day. We could leave early and have lunch there and in the evening go to the "Son et lumière" at Canterbury Cathedral. Pa again refused to come but said I could take our guests. I suggested that if they wanted to go, it would be helpful if Pa came too. They had come to see him, after all, and I would have to concentrate on driving the car. But Pa was adamant. Now I was in a dilemma because I wanted it to be an outing for Pa. I thought it would be interesting to take our visitors to meet our friend the retired Singhalese prime minister of Ceylon, who had become a sheep farmer outside Canterbury; on second thoughts it would not be diplomatic to call on him because India and Ceylon had not been friendly since partition in 1947.

We had a high tea with boiled eggs to lessen the burden for Mildred. She would never allow me to help her in the kitchen and even with our visitors Pa had insisted that Lilian, Leslie's wife, should come in and give Mildred a hand. Lilian was wonderful with Mildred. She was a little deaf, so anything she did not want to hear she pretended not to hear. Mildred thought of herself as the boss lady, but in fact Lilian did exactly as she pleased, so they worked in harmony. The minister had evidently used his chamberpot in the night, which amused Lilian no end.

The time for the dreaded sherry party came and the minister to my relief realized that Pa had become uncomfortable in society. "Come, Godfrey," he said. "We have come to visit you. We will not go without you."

Amazingly Pa did not need much encouragement. He got in the back of our very small Austin with the minister's glamorous daughter. He was proud of the fact that he could slip nimbly into the back while the portly minister had to sit up front and even then it was a tight squeeze. Our visitors enjoyed the beautiful scenery of Kent, and Pa kept busy pointing out the quaint circular oast houses designed to dry hops, the hop fields, and the fruit pickers. Judith Scovil and her husband Basil gave us a great welcome. The weather was wonderful so the french doors leading from sitting room to garden were open. I asked the minister if he would like to see the garden. Outside one of the other guests came up to talk to him. The minister soon put the guest's social graces to the test.

"How much do you earn a day?" he asked. The guest was an eye surgeon who travelled up to London every day.

"That is an impossible question to reply to," the surgeon answered.

"Well, what is your net income?" the minister continued.

"My expenses are high." The eye surgeon tried to dodge the question but the minister was persistent.

"How much do you earn when all your expenses have been taken off your pay?"

I had to think quickly what to do. I looked to Pa for help but he was having a wonderful time laughing and joking with Judith. What could I do? I could not tell Pa I thought it was time we left now that he was having fun. He would say we had only just arrived and ask Judith if she thought we should go. Judith would insist that we stay because she would not want the party broken up. Then I thought of the beautiful daughter. If she would come and talk to the eye surgeon the two of us could quell her father's interrogation. I asked her innocently, "Would you like to come and see the garden?"

She was overjoyed for alas, she herself was being unpleasantly questioned by the eye surgeon's wife. The three of us went outside, where the conversation became more conventional; we enjoyed the flowers, the view, and the weather and discussed holidays. The eye surgeon and his wife said they would love to visit India. The daughter rose to the occasion and told them the best time of year to visit and what cities would be the most interesting to see. I saw Basil, Judith's husband, looking tired and I felt we had really outstayed our welcome. I suggested to Pa that we leave.

"Oh no! Not yet," he answered.

Soon, however, the minister said he had had enough and thought he should return for his siesta. I offered to take him home and leave Pa and his daughter at the party.

"Oh no," he replied, "they must come too." When the minister spoke to Pa he agreed that it was time to leave. We all set off in good spirits. When I had unloaded them from my car we dispersed to our rooms for a rest. Immediately the telephone rang and it was Judith. She was missing a linen napkin and wondered if Sir Godfrey had inadvertently put it in his pocket. He had.

The next day the minister said, "Godfrey, we would like to visit Canterbury but we are not going without you. I will sit down and read the newspaper as I would in India."

Thinking ahead, I had discreetly filled the car with petrol.

Pa came and spoke to me.

"Do you know the way?"

It was yes and yes to all his questions. He finally agreed to come. With very little discussion we set off. Pa was like a shut-in on an outing, he had so much enthusiasm for the countryside. We went through charming Kentish villages and skirted Sissinghurst Castle with its wonderful gardens.[29]

Then we came on the Dover Road and saw the Pilgrims Way as we approached Canterbury. Pa, having told us the age of every fruit tree we passed, now began telling us about the different sheep. I found a place to park in Canterbury and then we went to find a pleasant place for lunch. There was an interesting restaurant called the Copper Kettle, but when Pa read the menu and the prices, he decided it was much too expensive. He was so out of touch with prices; I couldn't remember the last time he had eaten out. I suggested a pub but this did not please the minister. Then I suggested the local hotel, but again Pa was aghast at the price. I began to despair, thinking that we would spend the rest of the day deciding on where we would have lunch. I persuaded the minister to return to the Copper Kettle. He agreed and his daughter, chatting to Pa, distracted him so that he did not recognize the original restaurant that he had refused to enter. We had a lot of fun during lunch and a most delicious home-cooked meal. The café was within sight of Canterbury Cathedral so after lunch we walked over to it. This was real history for the minister and his daughter. We bought tickets for the "son et lumière." It was now getting dark and the weather turned nippy. We sat on benches and when the minister sat down the whole bench nearly tipped up like a seesaw, lifting even Pa out of his seat. Pa thought this was a great joke but he wondered whether the bench could take all our weight and moved to the bench behind. He enjoyed himself chatting to some of the locals. The "son et lumière" was wonderfully performed and the sound and lighting effects were first class. I drove home with the sound of the horses' hooves clip-clopping on the cobbled streets as we had heard them in the show. The next morning I took the minister and his daughter to Maidstone railway station. They had had a wonderful time and I was so grateful to them for bringing so much pleasure to my father. Then I returned the car to Pa, took the bus into Maidstone, and caught a later train to London.

Postscript

Following in Pa's Footsteps

Ziarat Hills[30]

If I must die then let me live,
When I have died, among these hills
And listen to the Winds who give
Their comfort strange which sorrow stills.

And let me move upon the heights
And see in all his splendour rise,
The Sun, who with his beauty lights
The snow which on the hill top lies.

And let me come into the vale
And let me tread the quiet way

Where shadows live and where the pale
Soft light of evening mourns the day.
And I shall find a treasure rare,
In finding which all troubles cease
A treasure rich beyond compare
For that which I shall find is Peace.
G.D.

Pa believed that if everyone wrote their problems on a piece of paper, placed them in a hat, and passed the hat around to others to exchange problems, people would be relieved to have their own problems back. Throughout my life this has helped me in difficult times, whether in India, England, or Canada.

In September 1973, five years after Pa's death in August 1968, I immigrated to Canada to take up a position as a teaching assistant in the Faculty of Rehabilitation Medicine, Department of Occupational Therapy, at the University of Alberta in Edmonton. Canada uncorked me, for which I am grateful. The Rockies brought back memories of the Himalayas in Kashmir, in the days before partition turned Kashmir into a battleground.

In February 1990, twenty-five years after my father's last visit to India, I went to Gujarat and stayed with our friends the Ambalals in Ahmedabad. Their home comprised three houses in a private compound. I stayed in one house with Leena Sarabhai and her son, Kamal Mangaldas. At night there was a constant traffic of rickshaws, buses, bicycles, scooters, and pedestrians on the street alongside the compound, creating non-stop noise. This initially kept me awake and the vibration made me feel as though my bed was being driven along the road. Over and above this noise I was conscious of a murmured conversation close at hand. I looked out of my window into the blackness of the night and saw the glowing embers of a small fire in the courtyard below. Two night watchmen were

Retirement gave me time to devote to my hobby of raising canaries, birds of my childhood.

squatting on their haunches raking the fire to keep warm. Their voices were soothing altos compared to the strident sopranos of the noisy traffic.

I often accompanied Leena to her school, Shreyas, where I would have an impromptu chat with three or four children: they taught me Gujarati and I taught them English. Students who have left the school still keep in touch with Leena. A little girl who was attending Shreyas was my guide and one day she took me to visit Gandhi's ashram. On another occasion, a student of Indian music took me to dinner and then to a concert. The music had a trancelike effect on the audience, and everyone nodded their heads in unison with the music. The famous sitar players began their concert at 7:30 P.M. and continued until two in the morning. None of the audience moved and I marvelled at their resilience: sitting on the floor was not the most comfortable way to listen to music. It was a memorable event. Leena had given me a plastic bag to keep my shoes in as everyone had to take their shoes off on entering the building. One of her nephews, who was on holiday from the United States where he was attending an American university, was also at the concert. He left his lace-up leather shoes (which, though worn by most in the West, were a rare luxury in India) with the chapals (Indian sandals) and miscellaneous assortment of shoes at the entrance. At the end of the concert his shoes were nowhere to be found. He went the next day to the bazaar where stolen items are frequently sold, but he never found his good leather shoes.

There was an 11:00 P.M. curfew in operation because of tensions between Moslems and Hindus who, given the opportunity, might start shooting each other in the streets. I was unaware of this until the journey home when I commented on the emptiness of the streets, which were usually bustling twenty-four hours a day. My companion told me that there were so many curfews that he ignored them all. On my last visit, thankfully we were free to gallivant at all hours as there was no religious strife.

Upon Ambalal's death, his house became a textile museum. Students who attend the famous textile college in Ahmedabad volunteer their time to take the public on tours of the museum. Some members of the Sarabhai family were still living in their compound in the beautiful houses designed by Le Corbusier in 1955.

After I retired in 1993 I returned to India, taking a bus tour of the Golden Triangle: Delhi, Jaipur, and Agra. While I was in Jaipur I telephoned Leena and she invited me to come back another year and be her guest. From Agra our tour flew to Colombo, the capital of Sri Lanka, where we boarded a Swan Hellenic ship that went up the coast of India and across the Indian Ocean to Oman. We had a special few days exploring Oman before boarding an aeroplane to London.

My last trip to India was in the millennium year. We went from London to Bombay where our Swan Hellenic tour joined the *Minerva*, which went down the coast to Colombo and up to Calcutta. Here I left the ship and flew to Ahmedabad. I stayed with Leena, who arranged for me to visit the textile museum where her sister, Gira Sarabhai, is the curator. Gira had arranged for me to see the correspondence that had taken place between Ambalal and my father from 1920 to 1970. In his letters my father remarked upon the longevity of their friendship, lasting as it did through two world wars and India's independence.

During my stay I took part in a one-day heritage walking tour of Ahmedabad. I visited Gandhi's ashram again where there is a school for untouchables, a paper-making centre, institutions for educating teachers and engineers, one of whom was a young Canadian, Chantelle Leidl, who is now my friend. Alternative methods of sanitation were also taught, along with methods of water conservation and techniques for harnessing solar energy.

I spent time with Leena at her school, Shreyas, where two or three of the children gathered around and once again taught me Gujarati while I taught them English. Time for farewells came too soon but there was the hope of returning the next year to Ahmedabad. I stopped in London en route to Canada. I had scarcely recovered from jet lag when I was shocked by the news of the horrendous earthquake that devastated Ahmedabad and the surrounding area on Friday, 26 January 2001. I telephoned Ahmedabad and to my relief I made contact with Leena. Her home, immediate family, and Shreyas were safe but twenty thousand people had died in the destruction. I was saddened at the thought of all those who had died and at the hardships the survivors would have to endure.

═══

When India gained her independence and Pa retired, his fellow judges, both Hindu and Moslem, begged him to stay on because they trusted him. But Pa knew that without the backing of the Crown any decision he made in a case between Hindus and Moslems in which one side or the other disagreed with his verdict could trigger a riot that might result in many deaths. His Indian judges continued to write to him in England. The ending of one letter from Judge Desaar was tearstained and barely legible, so saddened was he by the deterioration of the justice system. Pa's dreams for India were also shattered. He believed, like Gandhi, that a country can never be divided on religious grounds and that partition was the greatest betrayal for which the British had ever been responsible.

Salaam Namaste Shalom Blessings

Wendy Davis, Edmonton, April 2008.

Notes

1 Tobias Matthay (1858–1945), pianist and composer, taught advanced piano at the Royal Academy of Music in London for more than fifty years. Internationally known for his books on technique, he had many students who became famous in their own right.

2 Myra Hess (1890–1965), later Dame Myra, studied piano with Tobias Matthay. An innovative interpreter of the classics, she is best known and loved for the long series of lunchtime concerts she organized throughout the war. Held at the National Gallery, the concerts drew Londoners by the thousands.

3 Sir Walter Parratt (1841–1924) was one of Britain's foremost organists, known particularly for his interpretations of Bach. Long a professor of music at Oxford, he was knighted in 1892 and made Master of the Queen's (later King's) Music in 1893, a position he held until his death.

4   The Bombay Presidency was a large administrative area originally established
    in the seventeenth century to facilitate the operations of the British East India
    Company. Eventually it expanded into a huge territory that was broken into
    separate provinces, Gujarat and Sind among them, following the Government
    of India Act, passed by the British Parliament in 1935.

5   Gandhi was released in 1924 after two years, in need of an appendectomy.

6   Gandhi was arrested during the Salt March of 1930 and again in 1932, over
    the threat of civil disobedience; both times he was held at the Yeravada jail
    in Ahmedabad.

7   Mirabehn, born Madeline Slade (1892–1982), was the daughter of a British
    admiral. She went to India at the age of thirty-three after reading a biography
    of Gandhi, joined his ashram at Sabarmati, and became his closest disciple.
    Gandhi gave her the name Mirabehn, after Mirabai, the great devotee of
    Lord Krishna.

8   Gandhi went to England in 1931 to represent the Indian Congress at the sec-
    ond of three Round Table conferences (1930–32) attempting to resolve the
    constitutional issues obstructing the cause of Indian independence. This was
    the only time Gandhi left India after his return from South Africa in 1915.

9   Britain, France, and Italy signed the Munich Agreement with Germany on 30
    September 1938, allowing Germany to annex Czechoslovakia's Sudetenland
    in an attempt to limit Hitler's expansionist aims. With this gesture of appease-
    ment British prime minister Neville Chamberlain hoped to maintain "peace
    in our time." Hitler soon violated the agreement.

10 Ben Herman returned to England with his family after the war and joined the
    British Marines. In the 1960s he became equerry to Prince Philip. When asked
    what happened when something went wrong, he replied, "Things don't go
    wrong."

11 Elspet Gray went on to become a star in the theatres of London's West End,
    after studying at the Royal Academy of Dramatic Art (RADA). In 1949 she

married Brian Rix, who had started a theatre company in 1947 specializing in the farces for which he became famous. Rix was much involved in work for the mentally handicapped, for which he was knighted in 1986. He and Elspet had four children, one of whom, their daughter Louisa, also became an actress.

12 Frank Ludlow (1885–1972), a Cambridge-educated natural scientist and botanist, spent most of his working life in India and Tibet as an officer, teacher, civil servant, and naturalist. In 1929 he met Major George Sherriff (1898–1967), plant hunter and botanist, at Kashgar, where Sherriff was vice-consul. In the 1930s and again after the second war, they collected plants in Tibet and Kashmir, shipping many thousands of specimens to the West, many of them new introductions. Both men were keen ornithologists and Ludlow's collection of nearly seven thousand bird specimens is housed at the Natural History Museum in London. After an expedition to Bhutan in 1949, both men returned to the UK, Sherriff to a house in Scotland, where he created a Himalayan garden, Ludlow to botanical research at the British Museum.

13 From "The Kashmiri Song," by Amy Woodford-Finden (1860–1919).

14 The Shalimar Gardens near Srinagar were built in 1616 by the emperor Jehangir to celebrate his wife. They were the first of several gardens of that name built by various Mogul rulers in the seventeenth century. The Moguls ruled India from the early sixteenth to the mid-nineteenth century.

15 The exams for the school leaving certificates were sent back to England to be graded. During the war the exams had to be written in duplicate, using carbon paper, so that if the ship bearing the papers was torpedoed, copies could be produced.

16 Spike Milligan (1918–2002), Irish comedian, writer, musician, poet, and playwright, first came to fame, along with Peter Sellers, Harry Secombe, and others, on British radio's "Goon Show," which ran from 1951 until 1960.

17 There were more than five hundred "princely states" in India, ruled by maharajahs, khans, and nawabs. These states had never come under direct

British rule but had separate agreements and arrangements with the imperial Crown. They granted the British access to their lands, for example to lay rail lines and establish postal services, and in turn most states were allowed to maintain their own armed forces. After partition on 14 August 1947 the princely states were required to choose whether to join India or Pakistan. They were to cede certain of their rights and powers, principally their military capability, to whichever country they chose in exchange for a measure of sovereignty. The maharajah of Kashmir hesitated, hoping to negotiate independence. Pakistan tried to establish a claim on the largely Muslim state by sending in troops. Kashmir's Hindu ruler then chose India, which sent in troops of its own. After this first war over Kashmir the state was dismantled and has been occupied by the two countries ever since. The kingdom of Nepal, which had had commercial treaties with Britain since 1796, was formally recognized by Britain as independent in 1923.

18   During his twenty-five years in Burma, Colonel J.H. Williams observed the elephants that were used to haul teak. This book, first published in London by Rupert Hart-Davis in 1950, is the result.

19   The controversial Major General Orde Charles Wingate (1903–1944) led the Chindits, a special force of British infantry, Ghurkas, and Burmese Rifles, in two campaigns against the Japanese in 1943 and 1944. Using guerilla tactics, they managed to penetrate behind Japanese lines in the Burmese jungles, something that Allied forces in the area had considered impossible. Wingate and the Chindits were thus able to thwart the Japanese offensive against India. "Chindit" derives from the Burmese word for the mythical winged lions that guard Buddhist temples.

20   From "To a Bulldog," by J.C. Squire, W.H.S., Captain (Acting Major), RAF, killed on 12 April 1917. In *An Anthology of Modern Verse*, 28th school edition (London: Methuen, 1937).

21   During the two world wars pigeons were used by the British, American, and

Australian armed forces to carry messages, maps, photographs, and even cameras and to conduct espionage operations. The birds, which often flew through heavy shelling and clouds of poison gas, are credited with having saved thousands of Allied lives in the wars, and many of them were honoured for their valour. They are still occasionally used in military conflicts.

22 General Sir Claude Auchinleck (1884–1981) commanded the Eighth Army in North Africa between 1941 and August 1942. His success against Erwin Rommel's forces at the First Battle of El Alamein in July 1942 is considered to have turned the war in the desert around for the Allies. In June 1943 "The Auk" succeeded Lord Wavell as commander in chief of British troops in India. He was knighted and promoted to field marshall in June 1945.

23 In March 1947, as British control was crumbling and India's political leaders failed to come to terms, Prime Minister Clement Attlee replaced Wavell with Lord Mountbatten, who shared Attlee's belief that the British should leave India to itself as soon as possible. Having decided that the partition of India into two states along religious lines was inevitable, Mountbatten and Attlee were determined to achieve independence by June 1948. Without consulting Attlee, Mountbatten subsequently amended the date at a press conference, declaring that the British would relinquish their rule no later than midnight, 14 August 1947, a date picked more or less at random. The wisdom of such a hasty departure on Britain's part has been debated ever since; Mountbatten later claimed that he had hurried the date of independence in the hope of stemming the appalling sectarian violence that was spreading throughout India. While the violence continued, Mountbatten's abbreviated timetable eliminated the already slim chance for an orderly transfer of power, as well as any possibility of handing a unified country over to India's new rulers.

24 In 1935 Britain had passed the Government of India Act, which gave the country significant self-governing powers as a step towards full independence. By the war years independence was no closer; nor had the various Indian

political and religious factions managed to reconcile their demands. Meanwhile, British expectations of Indian support during the war had created considerable bad feeling among the subject population. In March 1942, when British control and prestige were at their weakest, members of the Indian Congress, following Gandhi's lead, rejected Britain's latest offer in negotiations towards independence: that Congress be given immediate representation on the Viceroy's Council with full independence to follow after the war. A few weeks later Gandhi declared that the British presence in India was a provocation to the Japanese in Burma and demanded that the British leave immediately. When Britain didn't respond, he coined the slogan "Quit India," setting off a wave of civil disobedience whose more extreme and violent proponents brought the country near to revolution.

25 Mohammed Ali Jinnah was head of the Muslim League. Jawaharlal Nehru, head of the Indian Congress, wanted a united secular federation that included the largely sovereign princely states, Kashmir among them. Like Nehru, Gandhi was against the partitioning of India along religious lines.

26 Between 1945 and 1949 a series of trials were held in Nuremberg, Germany, to prosecute members of the Nazi regime, many of them prominent, for war crimes. Numerous civilians were also tried at Nuremberg. The prosecuting countries were Britain, France, Russia, and the United States.

27 Joseph Emberton (1889-1956) was widely considered to be the premier London architect of his day, and possibly the first modernist architect in Britain. He designed prolifically during the 1930s and acquired an international reputation. Several of his buildings survive.

28 "Behen" is a term of respect meaning sister.

29 Sissinghurst Castle is famous for its gardens, designed principally in the 1930s by its owners, the writer Vita Sackville-West and her diplomat husband, Sir Harold Nicolson.

30 Sir Godfrey wrote this poem as a young man when he was newly in India, at the outset of the First World War.